The Covenanters

The Covenanters

THE NATIONAL COVENANT AND SCOTLAND

DAVID STEVENSON

THE SALTIRE SOCIETY
1988

The publisher acknowledges the financial assistance of the Scottish
Arts Council in the publication of this book

In the publication of this book
The Saltire Society acknowledg
the financial assistance of
The Drummond Trust
3 Pitt Terrace
Stirling

Designed and produced by
Fianach Lawry Associates/Ruari McLean
Printed in Scotland by
Lindsay & Co. Ltd., Edinburgh

Contents

For Gill, Mike, and 'KDEA'

1
Scotland's 'Marriage with God'

FOR MANY Scots Wednesday, 28 February 1638 was 'the glorious marriage day of the Kingdom with God'. At about four o'clock in the afternoon many of Scotland's noblemen assembled in Greyfriars Church in Edinburgh, where large numbers — probably hundreds — of lairds had already gathered. The document which was soon to become known as the 'National Covenant' had already been read to these landed gentlemen by one of its authors, the lawyer Archibald Johnston of Wariston, and prayers had been said by his co-author, Alexander Henderson, minister of Leuchars in Fife. When the nobles arrived they began to sign the great three-foot-square sheet of parchment on which Wariston had written out the text of the Covenant, and they were followed by the lairds. Signing continued until about eight o'clock. The next morning leading nobles took the Covenant to the Tailors' Hall in the Cowgate, where parish ministers were meeting, and nearly three hundred of them signed. Representatives of many, perhaps most, of the country's main towns (the royal burghs) signed in the afternoon. On 2 March Johnston read the Covenant in the College or Trinity Kirk (serving the North East parish of the capital) to 'the people of Edinburgh', and signing by the common people of the city continued all that day and the next. Several different copies of the Covenant were probably involved in these events, and many more were hastily written on parchment for distribution round the country — though most were signed by noblemen (and sometimes others) before being sent out, this being designed to encourage men in the localities to sign by showing the extent of support for the document.

In the weeks that followed copies of the Covenant were signed with enthusiasm in many parts of the country. In

1

many cases ministers during church services exhorted all present to swear to uphold the Covenant. After this the men in the congregations would add their signatures to a copy of the document — and occasionally a few women did so, though normally they did not sign. The many men who could not write had public notaries sign for them. In some cases swearing the Covenant was not followed by signing, and it is clear that not all signing took place in churches: some leading covenanting nobles and lairds clearly carried copies around and had them signed in their home districts or shires.

Covenanting zeal was most intense in the Lothians, Fife, Ayrshire and parts of Lanarkshire and the Borders, but there was considerable support in other Lowland areas as well, and though much of the Highlands remained hostile, in time Argyllshire and the northern Highlands showed support for the cause of the Covenant. However not all signatures were voluntary. It would have been a brave man who publicly refused to sign in a strongly covenanting parish, and in areas such as the North East where enthusiasm for the Covenant was limited expeditions of leading Covenanters, sometimes backed by military forces, travelled round extorting signatures from men reluctant to sign.

The movement which took both its name and its inspiration from the National Covenant was a great national one. Support for it was by no means universal, but the participation of most of those forming the dominant élites in society — nobles and other landowners, burgesses and parish ministers — and widespread support at the popular level provides ample justification for defining the movement as a 'national' one. And it was 'national' in another sense as well; central to it was the preservation of Scotland's national identity.

What were the threats to Scotland which inspired the Covenanters to rebel against their king? Why did the movement come to centre itself on a Covenant? And what indeed was a Covenant?

2
The Threat to National Identity

THE REVOLT of the Covenanters can be seen as arising from the long-term consequences of the two most important turning-points in the country's history in the previous century; the Reformation of 1560 and the Union of the Crowns of Scotland and England in 1603.

The Reformation of 1560 gave Scotland a Protestant church, but much more than religion was involved in the upheaval, for the events of 1560 saw Scotland reject her traditional alliance with France, as it was feared that Scotland was in danger of exchanging her status of independent nation for that of an outlying possession of the French crown. The cause of national independence having triumphed hand in hand with that of Protestantism, it was natural that the new Church of Scotland, which eventually won the allegiance of the majority of the population, should continue to associate itself with national issues of Scottish identity. Another 'nationalist' element was common to Protestantism in many parts of Europe: central to the Reformation was the rejection of the international authority of the pope in religion, the claiming of the right of nations to control their churches without outside interference. It was true that, in theory, the new church in Scotland saw itself as merely a province of what was hoped would emerge as a single international Calvinist church, with an international assembly as its supreme authority on earth, but in practice no such international organisation came into existence. Thus though Scots Calvinists continued to regard themselves as part of the universal true church of God, the highest earthly authority was in fact their own General Assembly, and soon this

national church came to have an important rôle in the
definition of the nation. Even before the Reformation some
Scots had argued that the (Catholic) Church in Scotland could
claim unique virtues arising from its antiquity and purity.
After 1560 such ideas were revived and intensified into the
boast that the Church of Scotland was the best reformed
church in the world, an example to others. In theory it might
be one part of an international body, but in practice it was
unique: Scotland might be a small and poor nation but,
mysteriously, she had been specially favoured by God to
provide a model for others. The way was thus prepared for
the development of the idea of Scotland as a nation with a
special, 'covenanted', relationship with God.

To outsiders, the inflated bombast of such assertions
seemed absurd, but the psychological forces underlying the
development of such ideas can easily be understood. A nation
all too aware of its weakness, of its relative insignificance
among the greater nations of Europe, bolstered its self-
confidence and pride by developing inflated perceptions of its
true significance; rather weak in worldly terms, uniquely
important through being chosen by God to play a leading
or *the* leading — rôle in God's plans for the future of mankind
and the establishment of true religion.

The circumstances of the late sixteenth and early
seventeenth centuries left the Scots very much in need of
mythology to boost their confidence, for 1560 failed to
provide a complete solution to either political or religious
problems. Where political independence was concerned.
Scotland had only been able to escape the French frying-pan
with the help of an English fire into which she was soon to
fall. English military intervention had been essential to
establish a Protestant regime free from French control. In the
turbulent decades that followed 1560, English intervention,
diplomatic and military, sustained that regime. As soon as the
young King James VI came of age he made a formal alliance
with England and accepted an annual pension from Queen

Elizabeth of England. Scotland was in grave danger of becoming a client state. But two circumstances made the situation bearable. Firstly, England might be the old enemy, but the two nations were now bound together by both having adopted Protestantism, and as the great Catholic revival, the Counter-Reformation, halted and then began to push back the Protestant advance in Europe, Protestant states obviously had strong interests in standing together. A major, if negative, element in national identity in both Scotland and England became virulent anti-Catholic sentiment. Thus Reformation drew the nations together, and made a pro-English stance one that protected Scotland's perceived national interests. Moreover, in the political sphere a momentous development loomed; James VI was the heir to the childless Queen Elizabeth, though she would never openly confirm his right to the English throne. Thus fears about Scotland's political dependence on England were allayed by looking forward to a Scottish king taking over the English throne, adding a political link to the religious common interests of the two countries. A Scottish king would preside over this link and, surely that would provide protection for the smaller kingdom in a Britain united under one sovereign.

A shared Protestantism had brought England and Scotland closer together, and the hopes of the Scottish reformers in the years immediately after 1560 were for religious uniformity with England. If realised, this would have meant that Scotland's brand of Protestantism could not have developed into a crucial element in the country's national identity: instead it might well have become a force in forging a British identity. But in the event Protestantism developed in the two countries in very different ways, and thus religion came to have a paradoxical influence on the question of national identity or identities within Britain. On the one hand common Protestantism and fear of Catholicism pulled the two countries and their senses of identity together: on the

other, the different variants of Protestantism which ultimately
triumphed north and south of the border pushed the two
apart, emphasising their separate identities.

The different forms of Protestantism which were to prevail
in England and Scotland can be linked closely with the very
different ways in which Reformation had come about in the
two countries. In England Reformation and (briefly, under
Mary Tudor in the 1550s) Counter-Reformation were
imposed from above by royal dictat. The result was in some
senses a 'conservative' Reformation. The new Church of
England recognised the monarch as its supreme head on earth,
royal power being exercised through powerful bishops acting
as the crown's agents. In church structure, beliefs and
worship, many features inherited from the Catholic past were
retained which were rejected by more radical Protestant
churches.

Among the latter was the Reformed Church of Scotland,
born not by royal decree but through armed rebellion against
royal authority. From the start the means of its birth gave the
new church a distinctive flavour, and in its early years the
new church was left, to a far greater extent than its English
counterpart, to develop as an autonomous body. Some of the
early reformers might have accepted an element of royal or
state control of the new institution, but circumstances
militated against such a development. First there was the
problem of a Catholic sovereign, Mary Queen of Scots;
obviously she could not be admitted to have any power over
the infant Protestant church. Then followed her deposition
and years of a weak Protestant regency (ruling in the name of
the infant James VI) embroiled in civil war against the
supporters of the deposed queen. In these years of royal
weakness the new church found itself able to evolve largely
free from state control. In retrospect it can be seen that,
whenever royal power was re-established firmly in Scotland, a
church-state conflict was all but inevitable. On the one side
was a church, born in rebellion and establishing traditions of

autonomy; on the other was state power determined to restore its authority and seeing control of religion as essential to this. Religion was too powerful a force for religious autonomy to be acceptable to the state: as in many other Protestant countries, the crown argued that the ultimate earthly authority in religion which had been wrested from the pope must be taken over by the sovereign, as God's representative on earth, if royal power was to be maintained.

The predictable conflict began in the 1570s, when the last of the regents, the Earl of Morton, sought to bring a church which had established a worrying tradition of independence under royal control, building up the power of bishops as agents in this great task. What was seen as state aggression led to clear-cut denials of royal authority over the church, and to moves towards outright rejection of any hierarchical officials, such as bishops, who might be manipulated by the crown in its bid for ecclesiastical power. Thus emerged Presbyterianism, claiming that the spiritual jurisdiction of the church was entirely separate from the secular jurisdiction of the state. There were indeed 'two kingdoms' in Scotland, and the civil kingdom had no power within the ecclesiastical one. Presbyterians accepted, in theory at least, that the converse was true as well: the church had no authority in civil matters. But in practice the dividing line between the jurisdictions of the two kingdoms was hard to find, and Presbyterian zealots often seemed to regard their spiritual kingdom as superior to that of the state. It was the state's duty to help the church when asked, and it was the church's duty to show civil powers (including kings) how to perform their duties in godly ways. Surely this implied the superiority of the church, and anyway how could church and state really be regarded as equal when the former dealt with matters of salvation and eternity, the latter merely with man's brief pilgrimage on earth?

Needless to say the development of radical and explicit Presbyterian demands for a church entirely free from the state, a church in which all ministers were equal so there were no ruling officials through whom the crown could control the church, in the eyes of the crown simply emphasised the necessity for bringing the Church of Scotland under state control. It was attempting to develop into a rival and even superior source of authority to the state.

The struggle initiated by Morton in the 1570s was revived by James VI from the 1580s. As James moved slowly to restore royal power after decades of confusion and weakness he was at first willing to try to compromise with the dominant Presbyterian faction in the church: a Presbyterian structure could be maintained provided blatant interference in political matters and challenges to royal power were avoided. But the intransigence of the Presbyterian leaders persuaded James that their power had to be destroyed, an 'Episcopalian' church structure established in which bishops (episcopus is the Latin for bishop) appointed by the king supervised the church in his interests. Most Scots of the time were not irrevocably committed to either faction in the struggle, and would have preferred some sort of compromise. On the one hand they might be worried by the more extreme claims of the Presbyterians, which seemed to threaten the order and structure of society, and were ready to accept some degree of royal control of the church in order to end conflict and restore stability; on the other many accepted and gloried in the developing national myth of their church as the 'best reformed' of all churches, and this myth was becoming attached specifically to the Presbyterian party. One aspect of the myth concentrated on the contrast between Scotland's church and England's, and took the form of proud boasts about the many remnants of the hated 'popery' which had been thrust aside in Scotland that were still present in England's half-reformed church, and about the contrast between Scotland's 'free' church created by a national movement, and England's slavish church at the beck and call of the monarchy which had established it. James VI's efforts to counter the Presbyterian threat by establishing bishops as royal agents looked to many like an attempt to anglicise the Church of Scotland, destroying some of its unique features and introducing 'English' corruptions.

Nonetheless, most Scots accepted that it was necessary to keep the wilder elements among the Presbyterians in check, and by the closing years of the sixteenth century James had won the initiative over his opponents in the church, though he had not completely defeated them. The situation was then transformed by the accession of James VI of Scotland to the English throne in 1603.

Again it is easy to be wise in retrospect and see the arrival of the Union of the Crowns as a disaster from the point of view of protecting Scotland's political independence and even her national identity. Yet most Scots evidently welcomed the news that their king was now also James I of England. The early decades of the sixteenth century had demonstrated to the Scots the potentially disastrous consequences of their country becoming an arena for great power rivalry. The 1550s had shown the danger of absorption by one of these great powers, France. Escape with English help had meant a degree of dependence on England, but overall the emergence of a stable, friendly relationship with her was welcome. Now further stability was to be added to the relationship by sharing a monarch with England. Scotland would be able to retain her autonomy: she would still constitute a state separate from England with whom she simply shared a ruler. The possibility of conflict from England, whose ability to devastate Scotland had been proved repeatedly down the centuries, would, hopefully, be ended for ever. Under the same monarch as England a minor European power would find a previously unknown security. Moreover, having a king from Scotland's native dynasty occupying the throne of her old enemy was a source of great national pride, and the fact that it was a Scot who would rule both kingdoms gave reassurance that Scotland's interests would be respected in the government of the newly-linked kingdoms. But beneath the surface rejoicing some probably had worries from the start about the long-term consequences for Scotland of the Union of the Crowns, worries arising from the disparity between the two partners. England had about five times Scotland's population, and the differences in national wealth were even greater. Would future monarchs devote equal attention to both countries? If their interests clashed, how would monarchs decide between them?

The very fact that it was taken for granted that James would rule his kingdoms from London provided the answer; inevitably England would be the centre and the powerhouse of the combined monarchy. James himself made it clear that he accepted the logic of English predominance, reassuring the English (needlessly worried that he might favour his native land) in 1607: 'when I have two Nations under my government, can you imagine I will respect the lesser, and neglect the greater?'

Thus Scotland's native Stuart dynasty, having inherited England's greater throne, soon pronounced sentence of death on Scottish assertions that the union was an equal one in which each partner had equal weight and consequence. Scots did not have to look very far either geographically or chronologically to see the possible consequences of a dynastic union of crowns for the smaller partner, even when the smaller partner had had the initial reassurance of supplying the dynasty. In the early sixteenth century the Hapsburg Duke of Burgundy, ruler of the Netherlands, had inherited the Spanish throne. Inevitably the new kings of Spain ruled in the interests of their great new state, leaving their homeland in the north to feel increasingly isolated and alienated. And culturally and linguistically the new dynasty was quickly absorbed by the Spanish court. The result was the revolt of the Netherlands beginning in the 1560s, in which a disenchanted people reacted to their decline into an outlying possession of the Spanish crown by attempting to restore their autonomy. The Dutch revolt was of great interest to the Scots, both because they had close commercial and cultural ties with the Netherlands and because Calvinism had emerged as the ideology legitimising the struggle of the Dutch against Spain, just as it had legitimised Scotland's overthrow of the French in 1560.

Whether any far-seeing Scot in 1603 pondered the Dutch example in assessing Scotland's likely future under the Union of the Crowns is unknown. But certainly within a few years some were finding it necessary to assert vigorously that the union had not made Scotland's relationship to England similar to Sicily's to Spain, or Ireland's to England — that of a subject territory. In effect, however, that was how many Scots came to regard the position of their country. James might retain a sentimental affection for some things Scots until his death, but he was very quickly converted to the view that in most things that mattered (not least in deference to a sovereign) England was superior to Scotland. Therefore Scotland's future should lie in being made as much like England as possible. James was probably an astute enough politician to realise that ruling over two such disparate countries was likely to cause problems: his solution was to whittle away distinctions between them with the ultimate ambition of merging them into a single political unit. In bringing about uniformity throughout Britain logic indicated that it would be easiest to bring the smaller kingdom into conformity with the greater — and anyway, in this case the king perceived the larger as providing the best model for adoption in his other realm.

The Union of the Crowns brought Scotland absentee monarchy, as the monarch and court were drawn south. Soon it became an anglicised — and anglicising — monarchy. This was most clearly and comprehensively seen in religion. Though in the long term ruling Scotland as absentees was to cause major problems for the country's kings, in the short term one consequence of the union was greatly to increase royal power. With his great new throne James' prestige was greatly enhanced, and, remote in London isolated in an alien English court, it was hard for Scots, whether nobles or Presbyterian ministers, to seek to influence the king's conduct in the traditional ways possible when he had been on the spot in his palace of Holyroodhouse.

Certainly it is hard to see how James could have got away with the major religious changes he imposed on Scotland in the first decade of the seventeenth century had he not been insulated from his subjects there by distance and prestige. His gradual gaining of the initiative over his opponents before 1603 soon gave way to decisive action. Leading Presbyterian ministers were lured to London and locked up or banished. Manipulation of the General Assembly's membership and business made it an instrument of royal policy. Bishops were restored to many of their traditional, pre-Reformation, powers. An act of supremacy explicitly claimed royal power over the church. Before this royal onslaught, resistance crumbled. True there were gestures of compromise. There was no attempt at outright abolition of the Presbyterian hierarchy of courts stretching from kirk session (parish) through presbytery (district) and synod (regional) to General Assembly (national). This has led some to describe the church James had forged as a 'working compromise' between Presbyterianism and Episcopalianism, but in reality it was Episcopalianism triumphant. Elements of Presbyterian structure might remain, but they had been systematically infiltrated by the power of bishop and king. If the essentials of Presbyterianism were an autonomous church and parity (equality) of ministers, then James' church, under his control through bishops, had little that can meaningfully be called Presbyterian in it. Individual dedicated Presbyterians, ministers and laymen, remained, but they were a leaderless, isolated, aging minority.

Though few resisted actively, there were many who were not entirely happy with what was happening, and from the first the way in which the king made no attempt to disguise the fact that in reforming Scotland's church he was anglicising it was seen as ominous. He might argue that this was because the Church of England had evolved in a way more pleasing to God than its Scottish counterpart, but to Scots, increasingly worried about the threat posed to Scotland's autonomy and identity by the Union of the Crowns, and proud of the traditions their own church had evolved since 1560, this was hardly a satisfactory explanation. The spectacle of some Scots bishops being consecrated by English ones might be explained by the need to restore the 'Apostolic Succession' in Scotland (the unbroken chain of consecration stretching back to the early church), but the implication that the Scottish church had abandoned an essential point of Christianity which was now being restored through England was unwelcome. Further, the establishment of a Court of High Commission in Scotland, specially designed for effective action against religious dissidents, introduced a name and institution copied directly from England. The restoration in name at least of elaborate hierarchies of clergy attached to the cathedrals emphasised to many that instead of the English church being purged of what many Scots saw as its disfiguring remnants of Catholicism, these were now being reintroduced to Scotland.

It was on the issue of reform of worship alone, however, that open and widespread opposition to James' policies appeared in his later years. The so-called Five Articles of Perth (1618) provoked such an uproar that James largely abandoned them and gave up further plans for reform of worship, though (to save royal face) the articles were not officially withdrawn. It may seem strange that reform of a few details of worship should cause so much turmoil, when the suppression of the Presbyterians and the wholesale reform of church government had been accomplished with relatively little trouble. But questions of structure and ultimate control of the church were remote from the concerns of ordinary parishioners. Changes in worship, by contrast, impinged directly on their religious practices, and the episode revealed the tenacity with which many adhered to forms of worship which had become firmly established since 1560. Furthermore, the opposition to the articles (especially that which demanded kneeling to receive the elements at communion) demonstrated the extent to which some practices accepted in the Church of England were regarded by Scots Protestants as not just English (though that was bad enough) but as popish — and there was nothing worse than that.

James' back-down over the Five Articles restored peace to the church superficially, but it may be argued that nonetheless they represent a blunder which had lasting consequences, for they represent the point at which, very slowly at first, Presbyterian sentiments, and even organised Presbyterian groups, begin to recover. Conventicles or prayer meetings, held to provide pure worship unsullied by the articles, continued to be held and formed nuclei of Presbyterian sympathy and organisation. Many of those, from nobles downward, who had led opposition to the articles were to emerge twenty years later as active Covenanters. Thus the articles may be seen as representing the point at which many who had watched the implementation of royal religious policy with reluctant acquiescence came to the conclusion that, as a few had said all along, the tendency of the policy was not just towards destruction of the unique purity of the Church of Scotland, but was gradually leading the church along a road whose logical end lay in Rome.

The anti-Catholic paranoia of many Scots in the 1620s and 1630s can be explained by the context of the age. The Thirty Years' War in Europe, seen as a climactic conflict between good and evil (Protestant and Catholic), created a highly charged atmosphere in which stories of great Catholic conspiracies, of Catholic atrocities, of open or covert subversion of Protestantism, seemed plausible — and indeed were sometimes true. James VI, reluctantly realising the fears underlying opposition to the Five Articles and how opposition could spread to other aspects of his policies, drew back from further religious reform. Particularly worrying to him must have been the fact that members of the Scottish nobility joined the opposition to the articles. James' destruction of the Presbyterian party had been made possible by persuading the nobility to support him against them, as their ideas could be regarded as threatening noble as well as royal power. The prospect of a new alliance between Presbyterian ideology and dissident members of the nobility was highly alarming. But for the moment James, by virtually abandoning the articles, halted the further development of such an alliance.

The Five Articles episode was not merely of religious significance. It was symptomatic of the developing problem of absentee monarchy, of the way in which James, in spite of his many years as a resident king of Scotland, was becoming increasingly out of touch with the climate of opinion in his native land now that he was an absentee ruler. Increasingly Scotland felt neglected and misunderstood by a distant government whose Scottish policies were clearly designed to ensure that in the long term there would be no need for Scottish policies, as the country slowly merged with England. Between 1603 and his death in 1625 James VI only bothered to visit Scotland once, in 1617, and though that visit was welcomed the fact that he used the occasion to press the adoption of various English practices on the Scots was not: the changes he wanted might be minor in themselves, but they were further evidence of his ultimate intentions for the country — that it should become a little England.

The part of nobles and other landlords in opposing the Five Articles may be regarded as the visible tip of the iceberg of a deeper malaise in the relations of crown and the great men of the country. One effect of the Union of the Crowns had been, in effect if not theory, to reduce a national nobility to a provincial one. The abrupt disappearance of the Scottish court

in 1603 had deprived Scots nobles of the centre of their
political and social lives. Few (unless holding high office in
the administration) could afford to live at the English court:
the conspicuous expenditure regarded as appropriate to a
noble there was beyond their means. Even if they could afford
to visit court the result could be disillusionment, for,
identified by their accents, alienated by the elaborate court
hierarchy and its formality of manners, scorned for their
poverty — and simply for their Scottishness — by their
English counterparts, the experience was likely to drive home
the message that their king had been captured by an alien
court. James, knowing the potential of his Scots nobility to
harm the crown, tried to flatter them and involve them in
government: but if they remained Scottish-based they were
likely to become frustratingly aware of their remoteness from
the real centre of power. Some had seats on the Scottish Privy
Council which still sat in Edinburgh, and on many issues
James conducted a real dialogue (by exchanges of letters) with
the council, allowing it to advise and influence him on policy
and its implementation. But sitting in council to receive
letters from the king was hardly the same as sitting with the
king in council to discuss the affairs of the realm, and there
were limits to the range of affairs on which the king was
prepared to take advice. The basic policies of anglicisation and
religion (up to the row over the Five Articles) were open to
discussion only in detail, and it was taken for granted that
'British' foreign affairs were conducted from London, in
England's interests. Scotland was no longer regarded as a
separate state when it came to control of relations with other
states.

James might in his later years have become out of touch
with Scotland, but on the whole he had the political
flexibility to avoid crises, or to defuse them once they arose.
And under him Scotland experienced a more prolonged period
of political stability than the country had known for
generations. 'King James's Peace' was recognised and

welcomed by his subjects. Nonetheless his political skills delayed rather than completely averted the crisis in the relations between the crown and its Scottish subjects which was inherent in the tensions created by the Union of the Crowns. Given the assumption on the part of the crown that Scotland's interests were subordinate to England's, and that Scotland should be anglicised, which were corner-stones of James's policies, an embittered reaction from Scotland at some point was highly likely.

If James succeeded in delaying a showdown with Scotland, his son seemed determined to hasten one. The explosion which became the covenanting movement was largely the personal achievement of Charles I. Immediately on inheriting the throne in 1625 he embarked on major policy initiatives in Scotland which strongly suggest that he was contemptuous of the way his father had ruled: the Scots had been let off lightly in the past, but would now be shown what royal power really meant. It can be argued that Charles' policies of administrative reform, limiting the power of the nobility, religious change and anglicisation were essentially little different from his father's. But Charles carried them to extremes and implemented them with a ruthless determination to get his own way whatever the opposition which changed the whole atmosphere of government. Reform of membership of the Privy Council seemed designed to weaken it by depriving it of some of its most assiduous attenders, and in general Charles made it clear that his vision of the Scottish council was of a body which executed his orders without question, and that for it to offer advice or suggest changes was impertinent. James VI had dreamed of absolutism, but realised that in the real world there were limitations to his power. Charles acted as if he believed that he actually had absolute power, and that his subjects would therefore obey him unquestioningly in all things. James VI had subordinated both General Assembly and parliament to his will. Charles never summoned the assembly and treated the Scottish Parliament with contempt: its function, like that of the council, was to support his policies without question. Even the traditional rights of subjects to petition for redress of grievances was no longer to be recognised: after the 1633 Parliament a noble, Lord Balmerino was condemned to death (though subsequently pardoned) for having a minor part in drafting such a petition.

To the two 'A's that lay at the heart of existing Scottish disquiet about the monarchy, that it was Absentee and Anglicising, there was now added a third: it was Absolutist. And there was one logical conclusion to be drawn from the king's methods of government. All customary and constitutional methods of trying to bring pressure on him were no longer viable (as he was a distant absentee) or were no longer accepted by him as legitimate. The only alternatives open to subjects with deeply held grievances were complete submission to the royal will — or open and outright defiance and determination to maintain this up to and beyond the point of rebellion.

Having shut off the safety valves which had allowed an element of consultation in government and permitted the relief of tensions through the expression of grievances, Charles proceeded to stoke the fires heating the Scottish boiler with a whole series of unpopular policies, abhorrent either to individual powerful élites in society on whose acquiescence his power ultimately rested, or to opinion generally throughout the community. His Act of Revocation of 1625 threatened to deprive the nobility of either direct control of, or feudal superiority over, vast areas of church land that had passed into its hands in the decades before and after the Reformation; to deprive many of hereditary offices; to change to their disadvantage the terms on which many held their lands from the crown; and to deprive them (and many lesser landowners) of rights they had acquired to the 'teinds' or tithes, the tenth of the produce of the land that was supposed to support the work of the church. If implemented in full the Revocation would have amounted to a revolutionary transfer of wealth, power and influence in Scottish society away from the greater landowners — and largely in favour of the crown. In the event the Revocation as implemented was much less sweeping, and even when landowners were to lose property or rights, compensation was to be paid. Charles' political folly was such that he probably calculated that making so moderate a settlement, after showing the full extent of the royal power he claimed to make or unmake the greatest men of the realm, would bring him their relieved gratitude. Simultaneously, it would awe them with what the king might do if he choose. Instead the Revocation episode created bitterness and deep suspicion throughout the country's landowning élite: if Charles didn't regard even rights of landed property as sacrosanct, it was unlikely that he recognised any limits to his power.

The attack on rights of property and office added an attack on the local and regional rôles of the nobility to the declining rôle in national affairs assigned to them by the new king through his government without consultation and his downgrading of the Privy Council. Moreover, increasingly Charles utilised bishops as members of the council and as holders of civil offices, to provide him with reliable yes-men in governing the country. James VI had persuaded the nobility that bishops were necessary in the church to maintain order and suppress the wilder Presbyterian elements. Now under Charles I the nobility found that the bishops instead of upholding the existing social order were being given a leading rôle by the crown in subverting it, by usurping power in civil government at the expense of the nobility. Not surprisingly many nobles decided that an Episcopalian church dominated by the crown was not such a good idea after all.

The exaltation of bishops in both church and state was only one aspect of Charles' plans for religious reform, which he

pursued with reckless haste after his disastrous visit to
Scotland in 1633. Charles had found that the Church of
Scotland conformed even less to his ideals than he had
imagined. Attempts had been made to express religious
grievances, and though these were suppressed they seem to
have aroused in the stubborn sovereign a determination to
teach disrespectful subjects a lesson by changes leading in the
opposite direction to those that they wanted. Not only in
religion, moreover, was the visit a disaster. Charles, a shy
man, had adopted the English court's strict formality of
manners to insulate him from those around him, and indeed
exaggerated stiff formality to a point at which it disconcerted
even the English. The Scots aristocracy traditionally had a
much more relaxed, informal code determining the relations
of men of differing status, and to Charles their friendly
informality — they were glad to see him, for all his faults —
seemed deliberately insulting. As a semi-divine figure the
monarch should be treated with a grovelling deference, and
this the Scots would not accord him. As a result, the king
returned to England regarding his Scots subjects as
unmannerly boors; while the Scots were horrified to find how
far, within a generation of union, their royal dynasty had
'gone native' in England. To all intents and purposes Charles
was an Englishman.

Charles' 1633 visit was followed by the Balmerino trial in
1634, demonstrating what the king might do even to great
men who questioned his policies. Two years later a new Book
of Canons, or code of regulations, was imposed on the
Church of Scotland. Quite apart from the contents of the
book, which were in many ways contrary to the traditions of
Scottish Protestants, two aspects of the book caused particular
unease. Firstly, the book was largely a reprint of an earlier
English Book of Canons. Secondly, the book was imposed on
the church by royal prerogative alone. James had had his
ecclesiastical reforms introduced by acts of General
Assemblies: these might have been in reality bodies chosen

and manipulated by the king, but at least the pretence had been maintained that the church's own assembly legislated for it. Now, in the church as in the state, Charles blatantly asserted his right to act without constraint. The absolutist anglicising of an absentee monarch was reaching new heights. Moreover it was already known that Charles, with his genius for not knowing when to let well alone, was planning to extend reform into the most sensitive of all aspects of religion, that of worship, undeterred by his father's burnt fingers over the Five Articles. A new Scottish Prayer Book was being drawn up, and like the Canons it was based on its English counterpart. To add further injury, it was no secret that the Archbishop of Canterbury was now the king's chief adviser in this as other aspects of religious reform in Scotland. The Scottish church was not only being anglicised, it seemed to be officially accepted that its church was subordinate to England's, that an English archbishop had a right to a leading rôle in its affairs.

Finally, not content with meddling with church government, discipline and worship, Charles added interference with basic theological beliefs. Central to Scotland's reformed church was the Calvinist belief in predestination, that man could not earn salvation through his own actions. Inherently sinful, all mankind would be damned eternally if God acted merely as a just God. But he was also a merciful God, and therefore he had elected some to salvation, to an eternity in heaven instead of hell. Those destined for salvation were so chosen before they ever lived, and thus the eternal fate of individuals actually living in any age could not be changed. This seemingly harsh doctrine, which can be seen as an extreme reaction to popular corruptions of late medieval Catholic doctrines which seemed to suggest that men could buy their way into heaven, had come to seem to Scots Protestants a central distinction between Catholicism and true religion. James VI had been as orthodox a Calvinist predestinarian as his Presbyterian opponents. Charles I, however, favoured a development in Calvinism called Arminianism which seemed to undermine predestination, and under his influence such ideas were reaching Scotland.

For many Scots the writing now seemed on the wall for their church. What has been called the 'creeping Episcopalianism', the piecemeal reform of religion in Scotland by James and Charles, now seemed to a great many Scots, and not just to a few fanatics, to be leading inexorably back to Catholicism. Charles would not explain his ultimate intentions: it was the task of a king to issue decrees, not to demean himself by explaining and justifying his intentions to subjects. But to his subjects it seemed he would not explain because he dared not. Even some Scots Catholics concluded optimistically that their king's destination was indeed Rome.

Tension was now mounting to near breaking point in Scotland. To the wider European context of Catholic threat was added the suppression of Scots Protestant dissidents in the north of Ireland and the onslaught on Puritan dissidents in England. There was an increasing feeling that somewhere, on some issue, a stand had to be made to reverse what was seen as being Scotland's slide towards Rome. And where better than on the sensitive question of worship? Conveniently the king signalled the imposition of his new Prayer Book well in advance, giving his opponents ample time to make their plans.

3

From Riot to Rebellion

SUNDAY 23 JULY 1637, it was announced, was to be the day on which the new Prayer Book would be introduced. Use would at first be confined to Edinburgh, so the capital's acceptance of the new forms of worship could provide a good example to the rest of the country. An example was indeed set, but one far from that intended by the king. In St Giles (raised to the status of a cathedral just a few years before by Charles' creation of the bishopric of Edinburgh) rioting began as soon as the dean began to read from the new liturgy. Riots continued outside: the dean wisely retreated up the steeple and locked himself in it for the rest of the day. The Tolbooth Kirk congregation, meeting in the partitioned-off west end of St Giles as their new church was not yet finished, also rioted. The minister of Greyfriars had to flee from his church, pursued by a mob of cursing women, 'he also cursing them'. In the Trinity Kirk the minister waited until he heard what was happening in the other churches — and then prudently conducted worship acording to traditional forms.

Outwardly the tumultuous reception of the new Prayer Book was intended to look like spontaneous revulsion on the part of ordinary folk at 'English-Popish Ceremonies' being forced on them. In fact the riots had been carefully planned, even down to the decision that women should take a leading part in the disturbances. It seems ironic that women, who were not (with a few exceptions) to be allowed to sign the National Covenant, thus began the riots which were to lead directly to the drafting of that seminal document. It was in fact quite common for women to be given this role in popular disturbances in European societies: it was a tactic which, presumably, was intended to give an air of spontaneity to events, and which made it more difficult for the authorities to impose harsh punishment on offenders, as they would hesitate to inflict on women the ferocity often shown towards male rioters. Certainly there were in this case many Edinburgh women ready to act, out of genuine religious conviction — though the name of Jenny Geddes as leader of the riots is not mentioned in any sources until much later.

How widespread the plot underlying the riots was is impossible to say, but a number of ministers and others were involved. It may well be that none of the nobility were actively involved, but it is highly probable that ministers who were determined on some action had sounded out sympathetic nobles and got a measure of tacit support from them. But though those who rioted were being manipulated by hidden leaders in the background, clearly there were strong and genuine currents of popular disquiet for the manipulators to work on.

The Edinburgh riots can be seen as an opening gambit: what would follow from it would depend largely on how the regime reacted. If it swiftly and effectively restored order and imposed its will then those in the social élites who opposed royal policies would not incur punishment, for outwardly they were not involved. If on the other hand there seemed a real prospect that something could be achieved, then nobles could emerge into the open and take over leadership of the movement, appearing not as the authors of a conspiracy against the crown but as society's natural leaders undertaking leadership of a national protest movement as a duty.

The reaction of the regime fully confirmed the hopes of those who thought something could be achieved. Charles' regime had seemed secure and unassailable; but one day of rioting in Edinburgh revealed the inherent weakness of absentee monarchy when it came to a crisis. Concentrating power in his own person in London, deliberately emasculating his Scottish council, Charles had created a system of government which worked well enough (from his point of view) while his subjects obeyed him. But once a crisis arose the fragility of the imposing facade of absolute power collapsed almost overnight. The Privy Council was weak and divided. Many councillors and officials were deeply unhappy at some aspects of royal policy, but Charles had seen no reason to replace them: provided they obeyed orders their personal worries were irrelevant. Thus when Edinburgh rioted the king's servants in the city were unwilling to take any decisive initiative to deal with the situation without consulting the king himself — which was of course a lengthy process as he was hundreds of miles away. When the king did learn of what had happened, as an absentee he was insulated from the realities of the situation, and it was all too easy for him to assume that he could still govern Scotland by issuing orders demanding obedience instead of addressing real problems, that what was in reality a highly dangerous development was no more than a minor nuisance in a distant province. So in the months that followed the riots Charles repeatedly and furiously ordered his Scottish council to enforce his will and punish trouble-makers. Yet this was something that the council had neither the political will nor the resources to do: the exchequer was practically bankrupt, the king had no standing army.

The king's intransigence on the one hand, and the lack of effective action to back up his orders on the other, simply stoked the fires of rebellion, and as a result defiance in Scotland spread fast. When the riots brought no concessions from the king a few ministers began submitting petitions to the council against the Prayer Book. Powerful laymen, led by the nobility then came forward to support the ministers' petitions, and a widespread petitioning movement emerged. Many nobles and hundreds of lairds, burgesses and ministers flocked to Edinburgh to maintain the pressure, demonstrating the widespread support for the cause among the social élites. In October the petitioning movement culminated in a great National Supplication. By this time frustration at the king's failure to make concessions was combining with happy incredulity at the extent of support for opposition to royal policy and at the ineffectual nature of the regime's response to crisis. The dissidents therefore went further in their supplication than just demanding the withdrawal of the hated Prayer Book. Now the Book of Canons was denounced as well, and a direct attack was mounted on the bishops, held to be responsible for these corrupt innovations. Denunciation of the Scottish bishops was genuine and heartfelt, but it was also a useful ploy politically. It allowed the dissidents to maintain that they were not attacking the crown, but the king's evil advisers. This formulation was one which allowed conservative-minded waverers to support the dissidents while maintaining they were not being disloyal to the king himself. Moreover, it had the advantage of allowing the king a face-saving way out of the crisis. The innovations could be withdrawn by the king, blame for them being attributed to the bishops rather than to the king himself.

Charles, however, refused to avail himself of this convenient (and traditional) stratagem for evading responsibility for his own folly. Yet he had no policy to offer except renewed threats of punishment for those who disobeyed him. His Privy Council was on the verge of collapse, discredited and despised, and could do nothing to stop his opponents evolving what amounted to an alternative government based on committees of nobles and others chosen from among the dissidents from all over the country who crowded into Edinburgh. In February 1638, almost six months since the troubles had begun, the king at last moved to break the deadlock. He made what he no doubt saw as a major concession: all who had come out in opposition to him would be pardoned for their past actions. But this was accompanied by a threat: future acts of opposition would be treated as treason. There was still no hint of concessions in religious policy, and, honestly but foolishly, Charles rejected the idea that bishops had led him astray. Responsibility for innovations in religion was his, and his alone.

This royal proclamation proved yet again that Charles had not faced up to the full significance and extent of the Scottish revolt. And this in turn persuaded his opponents that in order to retain the initiative and keep up pressure on the king they needed to go further than they had so far. Up to this point, in spite of the fact that they were now virtual rulers of much of the country, the dissidents had presented themselves simply as individuals and their respresentatives humbly petitioning for redress of grievances. Now, faced with the prospect of being denounced as traitors, they decided that it was necessary to bind themselves together, to each other and to God, in an organised movement dedicated to attaining their ends. The document through which they sought to do this was the National Covenant.

4

Bands and Contracts, Confessions and Covenants

THE NATIONAL COVENANT of 1638 took its form and content from a variety of concepts and types of document. First of all it was a band or bond, that is a written and signed agreement or contract. The word band was used of a wide variety of agreements, many very humble indeed (such as those relating to minor debts and commercial transactions), but in Scotland the word was particularly associated with written agreements defining relationships between individuals, usually men in the landowning classes. Bands between men of differing social status, such as bands of manrent (whereby a lesser man agreed to become the dependant of a greater one) and bands of maintenance (whereby a greater man agreed to protect a lesser one) can be seen as creating a sort of artificial equivalent of a feudal or kinship relationships, existing alongside them in the network of mutual obligations which sought to create a stable society of lords and their men in the localities. Bands of alliance or friendship between men of more or less equal status sought to stabilise relationships among lords.

The vast majority of these bands were purely concerned with local and regional relationships, but in times of crisis the signing of collective bands could be a method of consolidating a faction at a national level, those who signed agreeing to stand together for a common political purpose. Though 'banding' could be used against the crown's interests on occasion, Scotland's monarchs generally accepted the signing of local bands as a practice of positive value in creating stability. By the late sixteenth century, indeed, the crown was experimenting with its own 'general bands', whereby landowners in turbulent regions bound both themselves and their dependants to behave peaceably and submit to royal authority, and with political bands demonstrating support for the king in general or on specific issues. Thus in 1599 many nobles signed a band upholding royal power and asserting the king's right to succeed to the English throne. In the last decades of James' reign banding declined fast in Scotland, partly as the result of the growth of royal power; but, as the National Covenant indicates, the concept of banding remained strong.

Collective bands could be religious as well as political. In the years immediately before the Reformation of 1560 Protestant landowners bound themselves to act together to uphold the cause of true religion, promising before God to maintain his cause in sweeping terms, the phraseology of which is strongly reminiscent of that of bands of manrent and alliance. Later writers often refer to these religious bands as 'covenants', but this is anachronistic and misleading: the concept of a covenanted relationship with God was not present. In 1581 the religious band was combined with the concept of a confession of faith. Such a confession, a statement of basic beliefs, had been adopted by the new Protestant Church of Scotland when it triumphed in 1560, but a new type of confession was now felt necessary. There was a fear that Catholic influence was growing at court, threatening the new church. A document was therefore drawn up for signature by the young King James VI and his household stressing their wholehearted commitment to Protestantism and abhorrence of all popish errors. As most of the document was devoted to spelling out the Catholic errors that signatories rejected rather than explaining what they did believe in, the document became widely known as the 'Negative Confession' (though it was sometimes also referred to as the 'King's Confession'). After signature by the king and courtiers the Negative Confession was widely signed in the country on the orders of the Privy Council and the

General Assembly, and it was revived and signed again in 1590 as a test of loyalty to the new church and of rejection of the old.

The Negative Confession was a band which bound the signatories to each other in the common cause of upholding the king and his authority, true religion, the liberty of the country, and the administration of justice. Thus in 1581 the religious/political band had merged with the concept of a confession of faith. Still to take place were theological developments which were to provide the third ingredient of the National Covenant, the idea of special relationships with God defined in covenants. The Hebrew words usually translated as covenant occur in the Bible several hundred times, and are used to describe agreements, explicit or implicit, defining the relationship between God and man, or more particularly between God and his chosen people, the Jews. Through such biblical references the idea of compacts between God and man had long had a place in Christian theology, but usually a fairly marginal one. Then, in the late sixteenth century some Calvinist theologians began to give the covenant idea a central place in their teachings, resulting in the development of what later became known as 'federal' theology through use of the Latin word *foedus* for covenant — a word which could also be translated as contract or treaty. The numbers and nature of covenants varied from one writer to the other, but the theological teaching of the Scottish Covenanters of the seventeenth century was dominated by two covenants. By the Covenant of Works God had undertaken to provide blessings to Adam and his descendants, on condition of their obedience to the Law. But the Fall had rendered that covenant inoperative. It had therefore been superseded by the Covenant of Grace (or Covenant of Redemption) whereby, through Christ's sacrifice, God chose to elect some to salvation, rather than leave them to the damnation which the inherent sinfulness of fallen man merited. Blessings conveyed to the elect while still on earth through this covenant were faith, repentance, obedience to God's will.

The elect are saved through their covenanted relationship with God. But it was not the case that they won salvation by their own action in entering into such a relationship: rather the fact of their entering into covenant with God was evidence that they were among those predestined for election. A central psychological imperative within Calvinism, driving men to strict practice of their religion, was the need for individuals to find some way of convincing themselves that they were among the elect. The godly life, faith and repentance, the inner conviction of election, had added to them through federal theological ideas the reassuring concept of a personal covenant with God, part of the great Covenant of Grace, to which the individual could pledge himself.

Calvinism, with its emphasis on the eternal decree of predestination, could make salvation seem cold, remote, timeless, impersonal. Covenant theology was attractive to preachers because they could place predestination in the framework of the Covenant of Grace, and expound this to show that each one of the elect was placed in a direct and individual covenanted relationship with God. This helped to make the concept of predestination seem more immediate and personal, and it became easier to convey the particular obligations the elect owed to God.

There was one obvious danger from a Calvinist viewpoint in this sort of teaching: in trying to make predestination more palatable, was it not undermining it? Was a covenant really a contract, God offering salvation to the elect in return for faith and obedience? If so, free will, the ability of man to earn salvation through good works, might oust predestinarian determinism. Federal theologians strenuously denied the equation between covenant and contract, but in popular understanding it seems likely that the appeal of the covenanting idea owed much to such interpretations, and many preachers and theological writers were responsible, unintentionally, for encouraging this. In trying to explain the great, abstract concepts of the covenants they frequently made use of prosaic, down to earth metaphors which talked of bands, contracts and charters with God, often resorting to the phraseology of the law court and the market place, with talk of binding contracts with God and of sealing bargains with God. They might be careful also to stress the differences between covenant and contract. Man could not make a 'contract' which was binding on God, for that would place limitations on the absolute sovereignty of God: and the decree of election was not conditional on men keeping their side of a contract, for the decree was made before time began. Nonetheless, covenant looked very like a contract or band — reassuringly so, no doubt. As has recently been said, the old Scottish practice of banding was to reach 'its apotheosis in the greatest of collective bonds, the National Covenant of 1638' (Jenny Wormald), a clear indication of how the concepts of contract and covenant had become intermingled.

One of the leading figures in the early development of federal theology, in a European and not merely a Scottish context, was Robert Rollock, Principal of Edinburgh University, and it was through the teaching of Rollock and others that the abstract concept of the great Covenant of Grace first gave rise in Scotland to covenanting by individuals and groups. In 1596 ministers attending the General Assembly, alarmed by James VI's offensive against Presbyterians and fearful of Catholic plots, re-dedicated themselves to God and the exercise of their vocations. This was described as the renewing of the Covenant of Mercy and Grace with their God — though it was also called a 'league' with God. From the assembly 'renewal' of the covenant spread to a number of districts. The synod of Fife and the presbytery of St Andrews, for example, made a new covenant between God and his ministers, the covenant being expounded in legalistic terms as man's right, security and warrant from God, a contract, band or obligation between

God and man. 'Renewal' of the covenant was not confined to ministers; it was also renewed by many laymen attending the presbytery of St Andrews, and in many parishes as well. The Covenant of Grace was thus expounded in 1596, its relevance to issues of the day spelt out, and men solemnly renewed their covenanted relationship with God. But there were no written and signed covenants: renewing the covenant involved solemn public and verbal promises before God and men.

The outburst of enthusiasm of 1596 soon died down, though the covenanting idea was revived in 1601 when James VI, seeking to allay the fears of many about his intentions in religion, appeared before the assembly and, holding up his hand, vowed solemnly to execute justice and do nothing to prejudice true religion. Many were moved to tears by the king's eloquence, and they too held up their hands and vowed their support. David Calderwood referred to this as a mutual band of love between the king and the ministry, but also called it a mutual covenant, and the event was described subsequently as a renewing of the covenant by the king, orders being given for renewing the covenant throughout the land.

Thus by the beginning of the seventeenth century the idea of the central importance of a covenanted relationship with God was deeply rooted in Scotland, the great Covenant of Grace inspiring specific covenants or vows binding men to it, though verbal rather than written. In a further development the old myth of the unique purity of the Scottish Reformed Church was soon linked to the fashionable covenanting concept. Many of the covenants mentioned in the Bible were between God and the Jews, His chosen people. Through possession of the best-reformed church on earth, the Scots were in a sense the successors to the Jews, clearly chosen by God, awarded a unique status. The unique relationship with God must therefore be a covenanted one, for God had had special covenants with the Jews. Thus covenant ideas heightened the nationalistic element present in the Church of

Scotland, particularly in those inclined to Presbyterianism. Scotland was a chosen nation, the Scots an elect people with a great rôle to play in God's dispensation. Moreover, being a chosen people, specially favoured by God, put the Scots under particular obligations. If it was sinful for any people to accept corrupt religious practices such as those imposed by James VI and Charles I, it was far more sinful for the Scots to do so. As a chosen people their defection was the greater, the necessity of doing something about the situation to avert God's wrath all the more urgent. Moreover, surely this meant that once the Scots did start doing God's will, the unique status God had bestowed on them, the unique covenanted obligations he had undertaken to them, would give them victory, whatever the odds.

Many early seventeenth-century Scots believed they lived in an age in which the conflict of good and evil was reaching a climax. In the apocalyptic atmosphere of the age it seemed likely that the end of the world and the Day of Judgement were not far off. In this great conflict the Scots, singled out for some great mission, remained on the side lines. When were they to enter the fray? The unacceptable Prayer Book of 1637, the last straw in a seemingly endless series of corrupt innovations, seemed to many so ungodly that the time had come. The astonishing paralysis which overcame the king's government as soon as Edinburgh rioted, and the way in which from tiny beginnings the dissident movement swelled to a great national force with hardly a hand raised against it, confirmed this interpretation. Mere worldly action could not have led to such remarkable success. The hand of God was clearly visible, and it was now time for the nation to reaffirm its determination to do God's work by explicitly recognising and renewing its covenanted relationship with him.

5

The National Covenant

WHATEVER INSPIRED so many Scots to fight and die in the civil wars of the mid seventeenth century, it was not any stirring revolutionary eloquence or thrilling call to action contained in the National Covenant. Few who attempt to read it today are likely to persevere to the end without skipping some of the long passages in which it degenerates into tedious catalogues of Catholic errors to be denounced and of acts of parliament to be upheld, as devoid of emotive power as a shopping list. Even in its most lively sections the text displays no more than sober and dignified sincerity.

One's first reactions on struggling through the document might well be that the men who drew it up were highly incompetent propagandists, and that the Covenant must have come to be of such great importance through being a symbol rather than through what it actually said and how it said it. There is some truth in this. No doubt there were many 'Covenanters' who had only a very vague idea of what the Covenant actually said. Yet this is not the whole story. The Covenant's text is in fact a careful and well-judged propaganda statement, and the very features which seem most off-putting today were among its main strengths when it was first produced. The dry tedium of much of the text was reassuring rather than repellent. We may see the Covenant as the rallying point for a revolutionary cause, but the great majority of Covenanters welcomed it as demonstrating the opposite: that the cause they were fighting for was a conservative one. This is hardly surprising. Traditionally — in Scotland as elsewhere — rebels almost invariably claimed to be fighting to preserve or restore features of past government, society or religion which were under attack or had been destroyed. Their appeal in attempting to justify and legitimise their actions was to the past, either as it had actually been or as it was imagined to have been, an idealised golden age of earlier times. In denouncing the king's policies, religious and otherwise, his Scots opponents summed up what was wrong with what he was doing with one word: 'innovation'. It was not they who were trying to impose revolutionary change, but an innovating king. Their fight was to stop him and restore past ways of doing things. The reformed church in Scotland, once the most godly on earth, has been corrupted by royal intervention and must be returned to its past glory.

Most of the Covenanters were quite sincere in taking this 'reactionary' stance. Some, including Johnston of Wariston, were consciously forward as well as backward looking in their ambitions, however. Certainly they wanted to restore the church to the state it had been in at some time (never precisely defined) in the late sixteenth century, but they had ambitions to on from there to create a freer (from state control) and more powerful church than had ever existed in the past, and to use it to create a new society of unprecedented godliness. But such ambitions did not receive explicit expression in the Covenant. For them to have done so would have been counter-productive, alienating the very moderates who, it was hoped, would respond to the Covenant's massive (if dreary) appeal to the past and join the cause. Thus much of the Covenant was designed to reassure moderates uncertain how to act.

The Covenant's very heading emphasises this obsession with the past. It explains that the document is the Confession of Faith of 1581 — the Negative Confession — with a band added swearing to uphold true religion, laws and liberties, and royal authority. Thus at once the reader is reassured: this is no 'innovation', but simply the revival of an old and respected document signed by the king's own father and predecessor, plus a promise to support equally respectable acts and causes. From its heading the new document was generally known at first simply as the Confession of Faith, again a reassuringly conventional title.

The official interpretation of the nature of the document having been stated in the heading, the complete text of the 1581 confession is then given in full: and its incorporation into the new 'confession' emphasises the claim of the Covenanters that the threat to true religion which they were countering was a Catholic threat, and that the rightful authority of the crown was not being attacked: the confession had, after all, been signed by James VI. After the 1581 confession the appeal to legitimacy through the past is continued by an impressive list of acts of Parliament supporting the true faith, attacking Catholicism, ratifying the laws of the country, the liberties of subjects and royal authority — this last being endangered by the Catholic threat as much as true religion was. Significantly in one of the acts cited, James VI, while pressing for some form of closer union between England and Scotland, had guaranteed that this should not involve the laws and liberties of Scotland being 'innovated' or undermined, an obvious reference to the fact that they were now being threatened by an anglicised, anglicising monarchy.

The prolonged appeal to the past and legitimacy closes with references to the coronation oath taken by Charles I himself at his Scottish coronation in 1633. The Covenant then inches towards the situation existing in 1638 and action to be taken. Many precedents (including the Negative Confession) had established the custom of signing general bands for two purposes, defending true religion and maintaining the king's person and estate,

> the true worship of God and the King's authority, being so straitly joined, as that they had the same Friends, and common enemies, and did stand and fall together. And finally, being convinced in our mindes, and confessing with our mouthes, that the present and succeeding generations in this Land, are bound to

keep the foresaid nationall Oath & Subscription inviol-
able . . . ,

the noblemen, barons, gentlemen, burgesses, ministers and
commons who were to sign the Covenant had considered the
dangers to religion, the king's honour, and the public peace.
They had detailed these innovations and evils in their earlier
supplications and protests, and now before God, His angels
and the world, they solemnly declared that they would
constantly defend true religion for all the days of their lives,
and would refuse to practice innovations in worship, to
approve the corruptions which existed in the government of
the church, or the holding of civil offices or powers by
'Kirkmen' (ministers and bishops), until they be tried in free
General Assemblies and in Parliaments. They would labour to
recover the freedom and liberty of the Gospel, as they had
once existed in the land. The things they were complaining
about had no warrant in the word of God; were against the
church's earlier confessions and acts of Parliament; and tended
'to the re-establishing of the Popish Religion and Tyranny'
and the subversion and ruin of true religion and of their
liberties, laws and estates.

The way in which the past was being applied to the present
is now being made clear. By the Negative Confession and acts
of Parliament Scotsmen were stated to be already bound to
oppose the policies of the king: opposition was entirely
legitimate, a matter of defence rather than offence. The 1581
confession was a permanently binding 'national' oath — thus
introducing one of the words which was eventually to give
the document its popular title. Still more reassurance about
the un-revolutionary nature of the cause was felt necessary,
however. There was no intention, it was stressed, of
diminishing the king's power or greatness. Indeed signatories
of the Covenant would, to the uttermost of their power,
means and lives, stand to the defence of their dread
sovereign's person and authority 'in the defence of the
foresaid true religion, the Liberties and Lawes of the

Kingdome'. The official line was that all the causes mentioned in this sentence were entirely compatible, and indeed inextricibly interlocked: defending king, religion, liberties and laws amounted to the same thing. Yet the sentence was carefully worded so it could be interpreted in a rather different way: in undertaking to defend the king they would only do so insofar as this was compatible with religion, liberties and laws.

By this point the Covenant is adopting a good deal of the phraseology of traditional bands. Covenanters would devote their lives and all their resources in mutual defence and assistance in the cause of religion and the king 'against all sorts of persons whatsoever'. But significantly this conventional phrase is left incomplete: it normally ended by specifically excluding the king from the persons who might be acted against.

'Whatsoever shall be done to the least of us for that cause, shall be taken as done to us all in general, and to every one of us in particular'. No Covenanter would allow himself to be 'divided or withdrawn' from the movement by promises of favour or by threats: instead they would report the pressure being put on them. 'Neither do we fear the foul aspersions of rebellion, combination, or what else our adversaries from their craft and malice would put upon us'. Thus the Covenanters boldly threw down the dreaded word 'rebellion', because only thus could they make it explicit that they rejected its application to their conduct.

The Covenanters were binding themselves by a sworn band, legitimised by reference to the past, to act together, to stand and if necessary fall together. Central to the band is the fact that they are doing God's work, and the document closes by defining their relationship to God in doing this work. The Covenanters cannot, it is declared, hope for a blessing from God on their proceedings unless by their professions and subscriptions 'we joine such a life & conversation, as beseemeth Christians, who have renewed their Covenant with God'. Thus at the climax of the document, for the first and only time, the word 'covenant' actually appears in the National Covenant, which then closes by describing the Covenanters' understanding of their covenanted obligations:

> We, therefore, faithfully promise, for our selves, our followers, and all other[s] under us, both in publick, in our particular families, and personal carriage, to endeavour to keep our selves within the bounds of Christian liberty, and to be good examples to others of all Godlinesse, Sobernesse, and Righteousnesse, and of every duety we owe to God and Man, And that this our Union and Conjunction may be observed without violation, we call the living God, the Searcher of our Hearts to witness, who knoweth this to be our sincere Desire, and unfained Resolution, as we shall answere to Jesus Christ, in the great day, and under the pain of Gods everlasting wrath, and of infamy, and losse of all honour and respect in this World, Most humbly beseeching the Lord to strengthen us by his holy Spirit for this end, and to blesse our desires and proceedings with a happy successe, that Religion and Righteousnesse may flourish in the Land, to the glory of God, the honour of our King, and peace and comfort of us all.

A sentence with a structure so complex that it necessitates the use of twenty-nine commas seems distinctly indigestible today, but the gist is clear. Signatories of the Covenant pledge themselves not only to godly behaviour in pursuit of God's cause, but to godly reformation of their personal lives. So that those bound together by the band in the Covenant may adhere to it loyally (something which, it is assumed, inherently weak and sinful men would not be able to do on their own) and thus avoid divine wrath and infamy on earth, God's intervention is sought to strengthen their wills and bring them victory in His cause. The great and universal Covenant of Grace already binds God and men together and defines their relationship; now through their faith and dedication to His cause an additional covenanted relationship between the Covenanters and God is created — or rather renewed, for it is now assumed to have existed in the Negative Confession, and indeed to have existed long before that as a consequence of the Covenant.

There is a lot that is not made explicit in the National Covenant. The idea of a special relationship with God, not just of individual signatories but of Scotland as a whole, is not emphasised — though the Negative Confession has now become a 'National Oath'. The ambition of returning the church to an earlier time of greater purity is asserted, but there is no claim that that purity had been unique, that Scotland had a special, leading rôle in God's intentions for mankind. The covenant concept is present, but its full implications are not spelled out. At a more concrete level, there is some vagueness as to quite what changes are required in the church to restore its 'purity'. Changes in worship and government are mentioned in general terms. The attack on civil powers of kirkmen indicates a desire to move towards separation of the jurisdictions of church and state, but there is no explicit denunciation of royal power over the church, or of the office of bishop. The many civil grievances, such as those arising from the Act of Revocation and from arbitrary government, are subsumed under generalisations about laws and liberties.

This kind of vagueness was, of course, deliberate. In a document quickly drafted to unite Scots in the cause there was no time to work out detailed, concrete demands, a blueprint for a future settlement. Furthermore, it was assumed that Scotland's problems would ultimately be solved through a negotiated settlement with the king: to be committed irrevocably to very specific demands would make such a settlement difficult. Finally, and most importantly of all, the National Covenant needed to be vague if it was to unite the nation as far as possible behind the agitation against

the king. Being explicit on any of the matters listed above
would have been fatally divisive. What was needed was a
compromise document so phrased that men of very different
views could read very different meanings and implications
into it. To the most radical ministers and their lay supporters
the Covenant was a manifesto for religious revolution — the
complete destruction of royal power over the church, the
sweeping away of episcopacy and innovations in worship, the
establishment of an autonomous Presbyterian church. But to
have avowed this openly would have been disastrous. The
radicals therefore held their tongues and helped persuade
moderates to sign the Covenant by showing how conservative
and limited an interpretation could be put on it. That such
tact and careful phrasing was essential was demonstrated by
the fact that many of the ministers who were active in
opposing the king were at first reluctant to sign the
Covenant, believing it went too far — though the reluctance
of some, at least, doubtless arose from realisation that the text
contained deliberate vagueness and ambiguity, and from fear
of what the real intentions of the drafters of the document
were. It took a combination of reassurance and pressure from
the nobility to persuade many of these ministers to overcome
their scruples and sign, an indication of how close the
Covenant came to splitting the opposition movement and
becoming a symbol of disunity instead of unity.

Before it became known as the National Covenant the new
confession was widely referred to as the 'Nobleman's
Covenant'. This was entirely appropriate. The nobility were
dominating the other main élites within the dissident
movement — lairds, burgesses and ministers. It was they who
had decided that some sort of band and manifesto should be
drafted, changing the movement from one petitioning for
redress to one demanding changes and vowing to stand
together to bring them about. It was they who used their
authority in society to persuade doubters to sign. But they
had delegated the drafting of the text to Alexander

Henderson and Johnston of Wariston. Of the contributions of the two men, it is Wariston's which is dominant. Long before February 1638 his diary records him re-reading the Negative Confession, clearly regarding it as relevant to the circumstances of his own time, meditating on the Covenant of Grace, reading the works of Scottish and continental writers on political theory and resistance to kings. Once he and Henderson had agreed on the draft it was submitted to the nobles, and they and leaders of the other élites then made a number of changes before publication, to tone down some statements in the interests of preserving unity.

From its first signing at Greyfriars Church the new Covenant served its purpose well: the Noblemen's became the National Covenant as it was adopted as the symbol of a great movement that was at once *national*, because of the extent of support for it and because it sought to assert Scotland's identity, and *covenanted*, because it justified its actions by the concept of a specific relationship with God which determined how the Scots must act.

Some idea of what the Covenant meant to so many ordinary folk throughout Scotland is conveyed in the words of John Fleming, Session Clerk of the parish of Galston in Ayrshire. In 1640 it was decided to copy the National Covenant, as signed in the parish two years before, into the kirk session register:

> In consideratioun of the conveniencie of the thing itself,
> In thankfull rememberance of the singular mercie of
> God who was pleased to receave this land into covenant
> with himself, more formallie than any other people we
> hear of since the rejecting of his old people the jews,
> And speciallie of the late favour in takeing us home after
> our long gadding, and backslyding from his [God's]
> Majestie, And sealling the renewing of our Covenant
> with strange and sensible motions of his spirit in the
> hearts of all people universallie throw the land, And
> pouring upon us blessings of all sorts fra that day

forward. It is thought fitt be the Minister and Elders Gentlemen and others that the said Covenant quhich was solemnlie sworne and subscryved in this our kirk of dundonald upon the 25 day of March in anno 1638 yeiris being a day of solemne assemblie for that worke, and doctrein, with the wonderfull applause of all the congregatioun with out exception, shewing thare reddines of mynde by the elevatioun of heart and hand, cheirfulness of countenance, teares, and all expressioun of joy that the gravitie of the meitting could admitt. That this Covenant be recorded in our Sessioun buik among others *ad perpetuam rei memoriam*, that the posteritie may have this monument of gods mercy, this testimonie of our fidelitie in a corrupt tyme, this tye to bind them to the mantenance of the puritie of gods worship in all tyme . . .

Signing the Covenant, symbolising Scotland's coming home to God and being received into his special favour, was, in Dundonald as elsewhere, a highly emotional occasion, with tears mixed with smiles, joy restrained only by the gravity appropriate to so great an event. And, by the time John Fleming wrote his account in 1640, what were taken to be the effects of this national rededication to God were clearly showing themselves. With His help, little Scotland was already well on the way to destroying the power of the great King Charles I throughout all his kingdoms of Scotland, England and Ireland. The Chosen People were on the march.

6

The Scottish Revolution, 1638-51

THE EVENTS of 1638-41 seemed to provide a complete vindication of the stand taken by the Scots in the National Covenant and of their conviction that, with God's help, they could not fail.

Charles I's reaction to news of the Covenant was to acknowledge at last how serious the situation in Scotland was. He was faced by open, organised rebellion, and such had been the incompetence of his own and his agents' responses to the emergence of dissidence that the rebels effectively controlled much of the country. The king therefore concluded that force was necessary to restore order, and that the dominant component of such force should be English, since he had already lost most of Scotland. While preparations for use of force were made, the Covenanters would be lulled into a false sense of security by negotiating with them and making concessions to them.

These decisions were fatal to Charles' own interests in several respects. It quickly became obvious to the Covenanters that the king was intent on war: raising an army could hardly be done in secret, and the Covenanters were anyway kept in close touch with what was going on by sympathisers at the king's court. The dissidents had long stressed the patriotic element in their protests at the way Scotland was being treated, but now this theme became far more central than before: Scotland was faced with English invasion. To support the king, or even to try to remain neutral, became a readiness to accept the national humiliation of invasion and conquest by the old enemy. Thus the appeal to English arms by the king drove many moderate Scots into the hands of the Covenanters. Simultaneously, the king's willingness to make concessions, which he had no intention of honouring once they had served their purpose, necessitated a rethinking by the Covenanters' leaders of the nature of the ultimate settlement to be made with the king. Up to this point most of the leadership had regarded their struggle as essentially aimed at trying to get the king to withdraw unpopular policies, show more respect for Scottish interests, national and sectional, and rule with a greater degree of consultation than in the past. Obviously this would entail some degree of limitation of royal power, seen as necessary to restore it to its traditional bounds before the 'innovations' in royal power seen since 1603. Nonetheless, the hope and intention was not to destroy royal power. But now, it seemed, getting the king to agree to make concessions was not going to be enough, for he would never feel bound by promises extorted from him by rebellious subjects. As soon as was politically expedient he would withdraw them — and take his revenge on those who had extorted them. The fact that the king's word could not be trusted led the Covenanters logically to a momentous conclusion. Royal power must be so limited that in future he would not be able to revert to his innovating policies. As the logic of the situation dawned gradually on the Covenanters, so their demands grew ever wider.

Of course if Charles had found it possible to raise English armies capable of crushing the Scots none of this would have mattered. But he failed. Few in England were enthusiastic about a war with Scotland — and skilful Scots propaganda stressed that the Covenanters had no national quarrel with the English, and that they were protesting at religious and other grievances against the king which were shared by many Englishmen. Thus trying to raise an army in England met with widespread opposition, revealing that Charles' imposing regime was almost as fragile there as north of the border. He failed to invade Scotland in 1638, and at the end of the year the famous Glasgow Assembly met. The king had given permission for this, confident that by the time it met he would be in a position to dominate it. Instead it was packed, through carefully rigged elections, with Covenanting ministers; and many of their noble and other powerful lay supporters elbowed their way into a church assembly as elders. At this point the movement became fully and openly a Presbyterian one. Government of the church by bishops, the civil powers of churchmen and the Five Articles of Perth, were declared unlawful, and a declaration to this effect, the 'Glasgow Determination', was ordered to be added to all copies of the National Covenant (often above existing signatures!) — and subscription of the Covenant was made compulsory. Royal power over the church, Charles's Book of Canons and Book of Common Prayer and all other detested innovations were rejected by this 'free' General Assembly — free at least in the sense of being free of royal control. Thus the whole structure of royal domination of the church, built up with so much skill and effort by James VI, was destroyed within a matter of days.

Presbyterianism had triumphed. Or had it? A church structure completely Presbyterian in form existed, purged of innovations and with the General Assembly as its supreme authority on earth. But was it a church independent of civil control? In theory yes, in practice no. The nobility and lairds had originally been willing to support James VI's suppression of Presbyterianism, by infiltrating the church with bishops as his agents, as they shared the king's distrust and fear of extreme Presbyterian ideas, potentially harmful to their positions in society. Charles' use of bishops to help impose unpopular policies, in state as well as church, had led to such a strong reaction against them among landowners that they now supported their abolition. But the landowners had no intention of allowing the 'tyranny' in society of hundreds of Presbyterian ministers to replace that of the fourteen bishops. As elders, they would therefore infiltrate the Presbyterian structure to prevent it becoming a threat to the traditional order of society.

The religious revolution of 1638 was master-minded by an unholy alliance of a minority of Presbyterian zealots among the ministers with conservative nobles, the authority of the latter being necessary to persuade the more moderate majority of ministers to go so far as to abolish bishops. The alliance was effective in pushing through the revolution, but internal tensions within it stored up trouble for the future. The nobility and lairds saw the religious revolution as complete: bishops and royal influence over the church were gone, leaving a church which landowners could in the last analysis dominate as elders. They had got what they wanted. But for the radical minority of ministers revolution had only just begun, and they looked forward to the time when, no longer entirely dependant on the support of conservative landowners, they could push on to a really free church and create a new godly society.

In 1639, as in 1638, Charles I failed to invade Scotland. He got an army to the borders, but the forces raised by the Covenanters to oppose him were too formidable to attack. He therefore settled, humiliatingly, for a truce. This soon broke down, and both sides prepared for a new confrontation. But the initiative still lay with the Covenanters. In 1640 they held a session of the Parliament of Scotland, abolished the apparatus of royal control of proceedings, and passed legislation (assumed to be operative without royal assent) including a triennial act insisting that Parliament meet at least once every three years.

It has sometimes been argued that the fact that the Covenanters held a General Assembly before a Parliament indicates that the former was more important than the latter in Scotland, and that this demonstrates that the Covenanting movement was almost exclusively religious in its nature and motivation. This is simply not true. The assembly did meet first partly because the main specific grievances demanding redress were religious, but primarily it came first because it was taken for granted that its legislation would subsequently be ratified by Parliament. This was done by the 1640 session, indicating acceptance of Parliament's supremacy.

The 1640 parliamentary session added constitutional revolution to religious, asserting the rights of the three estates (hastily redefined since the bishops, representing the church estate, no longer existed) to act for themselves in the king's absence. But the confidence of the Covenanters was demonstrated even more strikingly when, after Parliament rose, they broke the long stalemate on the border by invading England, determined to force a slippery, absentee king to make a settlement. The king's English forces collapsed, the Scots easily occupied the northern counties, and forced the king to make another humiliating truce under threat of advancing further south. Their distrust of the king was such that they insisted that he summon the English Parliament to be a party to a peace treaty, so they could get it to guarantee that the king would not in future be able to attempt to mobilise English forces against Scotland. Moreover, a meeting of Parliament would provide the king's English opponents with a national forum to press for redress of their grievances, and thus embroil the king in a struggle with Englishmen who would seek to limit his power. Obviously this was likely to work to the advantage of the Scots.

At first this proved the case. Once what was to become known as the Long Parliament met in England and launched an attack on Charles's policies and powers, his perception of the Scottish rebellion changed. England was by far the greatest of his kingdoms, the centre of his power. Regaining control of it therefore became his first priority. The Scots threat was now perceived as being of secondary importance, and Charles hoped that they could be bought off with concessions: he even calculated, with his usual political naivety, that showing generosity to the Scots would win gratitude from them. They would demonstrate this by helping him against his English enemies! Inspired by this utterly absurd conception, Charles came to Scotland in 1641, gave his assent to the religious and constitutional revolutions — and indeed extended the latter by accepting that in future his choice of officials, councillors and judges would require the approval of the Scottish Parliament. He then appointed many leading Covenanters to high office, promoted some in the nobility, lavished pensions on many. In return he gained absolutely nothing: the Covenanters quite rightly distrusted his motives: if they helped him restore his power in England, obviously he would then use it against them. And soon Charles had to hasten back to London to deal with the disastrous news that a great rebellion had broken out in England's subordinate kingdom of Ireland. The Scots in one of his outlying kingdoms had demonstrated the brittleness of his seemingly unassailable power, and now the Irish were following their example.

From riots in Edinburgh in 1637 the Covenanters had moved on from success to success, until in 1641 they dominated both church and state and had forced the king to give his approval to this settlement. Their triumph was quite astonishing, and they had gone far further than anyone could have imagined at the beginning. No wonder some were intoxicated with visions of the limitless possibilities open to a covenanted nation to which God had shown himself ready to bring victory over what were, in worldly terms, impossible odds. With the king embroiled with his English parliament and faced with war in Ireland there was no likelihood that in the forseeable future he would have much time for Scottish affairs: so much the better, for the Covenanters he had left in power could consolidate their positions in the country, free for the moment from any external threat.

There, was, however, a massive complication. The Union of the Crowns had, in many ways, produced the conditions that had forced the Scots into revolt in 1637. But the circumstances of union had also helped the Covenanters to their triumph in 1641: had Charles been king of Scotland alone, resident in the country, he would hardly have agreed to the sweeping abdication of power he accepted in 1641. Yet it was the consequences of union which were to destroy the covenanting movement. Developments in England and Ireland had temporarily diverted Charles' attention from Scotland. But what would happen if in the future he regained power in England? Scotland could only be secure once her place within Britain was more satisfactorily defined than it was by the Union of the Crowns. The Covenanters recognised this, and in negotiations with the English parliament in 1640-1 they had sought to achieve a stable relationship based on religious uniformity on Presbyterian lines (how could the covenanted church feel secure while there were still bishops in England?) and, in civil affairs, a sort of loose federal union in which a joint commission drawn equally from each of the two parliaments would consider matters of common interest (such as foreign policy and war), act to prevent disputes between the kingdoms, and make sure that the king could not use one kingdom's resources against the other. These attempts at redefining the union had failed, as the English simply were not interested. But they showed that the Covenanters were worrying about Scotland's future within Britain. Events were quickly to prove how right they were to be apprehensive.

First the situation in Ireland called for attention. Though Ireland was a dependency of England, the Scots felt it necessary to intervene in the civil war there. The rebels, who looked likely to gain control of the whole country, were Catholics, and this threatened the many thousands of Scots Protestant colonists who had settled in Ulster since the beginning of the century. Ulster in Catholic hands, just a short sea crossing from western Scotland, would be a strategic threat to Scotland's security. Moreover, the Covenanters saw their God-given mission as destroying the Catholic menace: they had succeeded in Scotland only for the reality of Catholic conspiracy to be demonstrated in Ireland. Out of both self-interest and principle, therefore, the Covenanters agreed with the English Parliament to send an army of over 10,000 men to Ulster in 1642. But no sooner had one hole in the dykes protecting Protestant interests in the British Isles been plugged than another appeared. England drifted into civil war, with both sides appealing for Scottish help. In the early campaigns of 1642 and 1643 the royalists won repeated victories. Soon, it appeared, the royalists would overwhelm the English Parliament. Thus the Covenanters were faced with the nightmare prospect of King Charles establishing absolute power in England after military triumph, and then turning his attention to revenge on the Scots, whose conduct after 1637 had been responsible for destabilising all Britain.

In the end the Scots concluded that they had to intervene in England to protect their revolution: in the autumn of 1643 they negotiated the Solemn League and Covenant with the English parliamentarians. The latter wanted only a military treaty: the new Covenant was the price the Scots demanded in return for military help. As its title indicates, however, it was a civil treaty (a league) as well as a religious covenant. Religious uniformity on the lines of Scottish Presbyterianism was to be established in all three kingdoms, and popery and other religious errors were to be extirpated. The rights of parliaments and the liberties of the kingdoms of England and Scotland were to be upheld. England and Scotland were to be bound together for all time in a firm peace and union — which was vague, but it soon became clear that the Covenanters were reviving their ideas for a federal relationship in which England and Scotland would be equal partners. Finally, as in its predecessor of 1638, the new Covenant included a band binding its supporters to each other in fighting for their cause, and a covenant declaring before God their determination to fight for his cause, and seeking his help in this. Only after agreeing to all this did the English get the Scots to send an army of over 20,000 men to England.

The results of the Solemn League and Covenant were disastrous for Scotland, and it has therefore often been denounced as sheer folly, as arising simply from narrow religious fanaticism. This was certainly present. Opposing the king in England was seen as a continuation of the great crusade against Catholicism, and earlier successes had led to an over-estimation of Scotland's military potential. Imposing Presbyterianism on a reluctant England was justified as it was the most godly form of church government: and a few at least dreamed of quickly sorting out England's problems and then moving on to the continent for the final assault on the Anti-Christ of Catholicism. But alongside such follies went careful political calculation. Scotland had to intervene in England to protect her revolution from the king, who would otherwise triumph. And a settlement must be made in England compatible with that in Scotland. In the language of a much later and greater revolution (the Russian), Scotland found that the logic of events compelled her to try to 'export the revolution', as 'revolution in one country' could not provide lasting security. The gamble of intervention in England failed: but it is hard to see what else the Covenanters could have done other than wait passively until events elsewhere determined their fate.

Intervention in the English civil war nonetheless caused a major split among the Covenanters. Many, especially among the nobility, opposed it either on practical grounds or as an unjustified attack on a king who had granted them all they wanted. Moreover, having involved themselves in war in England as well as Ireland, the Covenanters were soon engaged in war on a third front as well. Intervention in England provoked royalist rebellion in Scotland. In 1644-5 the royalist Marquis of Montrose (formerly a leader of the Covenanters) led a small army of Irish Catholics and Highlanders to six successive victories over Covenanting armies. Eventually he was defeated, but the Scots war-effort in all three kingdoms was now faltering, and Montrose's early victories caused intense shock to the Covenanters, used only to repeated successes. What had gone wrong? Why was their God letting them be defeated by the forces of evil?

By the time Montrose had been defeated the English civil war was clearly moving towards victory for Parliament. The Scots army in England had undoubtedly tipped the balance in Parliament's favour, but it had not won the dramatic victories expected of it, so the Scots were not in the dominant position that they had hoped, able to dictate a peace settlement. Further, resenting Scots arrogance and the terms of the Solemn League and Covenant which had been forced on it, the English Parliament became increasingly anti-Scottish in sentiment. To keep the Scots happy while their military help was essential, Parliament accepted the 'Westminster Standards' negotiated with the Scots as a basis for religious uniformity, defining such matters as theological beliefs and forms of government and worship. But while the Scottish church adopted them fully it became clear that they would remain a dead letter in England. Thus ironically the Church of Scotland, which was to continue in the centuries ahead to claim to stand for a distinctively Scottish religious identity, had as its official standards expositions of beliefs, organisation and worship drawn up by an English assembly! In politics as in religion the Scots were disappointed by their English allies. Their attempts to have their negotiating terms adopted in dealing with the now defeated king and their demands for a redefinition of the union met with English hostility.

The bitterness in Scotland was intense. They had been betrayed by their English allies. Parliament had cynically accepted their military help and then, once the war was won, refused to pay the price promised or to admit that Scots intervention had change the course of the war. Humiliated by Montrose in Scotland, the Covenanters were now to lose the glittering prize of a British peace settlement tailor-made to guarantee Scotland's future security within Britain. These events of the mid-1640s mark the point at which the

Covenanting movement lost momentum and began to collapse. Deep divisions began to emerge as to how to react to the situation. Most of the nobility decided that the best way ahead lay in agreement with the king. Now he was totally defeated, surely he would accept their terms as the only way back to power. A revised union could then be based not on federal links between the two parliaments but on strong formal representation of Scotland in the king's court. Allying themselves with moderate royalists under the leadership of the royalist Duke of Hamilton, this faction negotiated a secret treaty with the king, the Engagement, in 1647. But the more extreme Covenanters, led by the Marquis of Argyll and supported by most of the ministers of the church, refused to accept the treaty.

In spite of this opposition the Engagers won control of Scotland and raised a new army. Thus in the first major confrontation between church and state since the revolution of 1637-41, the church lost. Many ministers were stunned. They had believed they had created a Presbyterian church strong enough to impose its will on the country in any matter relating to religion. Now they were contemptuously swept aside.

Events soon changed their fortunes, however. The Engagers' army was routed by Oliver Cromwell at the Battle of Preston after it invaded England in 1648. This left a power vacuum in Scotland, and Argyll and the more extreme Covenanters hastily raised forces and seized power with Cromwell's help. The new regime became known, significantly, as that of the Kirk Party. Not only had it the support of most ministers, but ministers now had much more direct influence in political matters than ever before. A few nobles, like Argyll, supported the new regime, but most had been Engagers. They were now purged from power, temporarily ending the political dominance of the nobility. Now the time had come, the more radical ministers believed, to achieve their ambitions for further reform, the building of a truly godly society. Under the Kirk Party the social attitudes of the Covenanting movement changed dramatically. What had originally been seen as the godly nobility had now betrayed the cause. Social conservatism gave way to attacks on the nobles and other larger landlords as corrupt oppressors of the poor commons, the true people of God who had been hostile to the Engagement. Radical policies were introduced designed to change the balance of power in society, while public offices, Parliament and the army were thoroughly purged to exclude all from power who did not measure up to strict standards of godliness.

In part this purging arose from political expediency, the need of the Kirk Party to consolidate its hold on the country, but it also reflected the party's perception of the situation Scotland was in. The great question to be answered was why God, after first bringing his chosen people victory in His name, had deserted them and allowed them to be humiliated by repeated disasters. The Kirk Party's answer was that this was God's punishment on them for compromising, for not pushing on with moral and other reforms in Scotland with sufficient zeal, for co-operating with English parliamentarians and (in the case of the Engagers) even with royalists, men who were not truly dedicated to the cause of God. The only way in which the Scots could win back God's favour was by purging all tainted with ungodly conduct from public life, and by pursuing policies designed to impose the strictest moral discipline on the country. The Covenanting vision, which had begun by embracing the entire Scottish nation as the people of God with a great mission, was being narrowed down to a concept of an exclusive élite of the truly godly with a duty to force the rest of society into conformity.

The radical policies of the Kirk Party, however, were not based on any fundamental shift of power within society, but on the chance to grab power handed to the party by the English defeat of the Engagers. Its hold on power was therefore fragile from the start. At first the Kirk Party regime maintained an uneasy alliance with England, where power by now was increasingly in the hands of Oliver Cromwell and the army. But this alliance was broken by the execution of Charles I and the abolition of the monarchy in England. In spite of its radical attitudes in some respects, the Kirk Party was genuinely horrified. The English might have executed Charles as king of England; but he had also been King of Scots. Moreover in spite of Scots bitterness at the anglicisation of the crown since 1603, the dynasty was Scottish by blood, and it had been central to Scotland's identity for centuries. Therefore the dead king's son was immediately proclaimed Charles II — and King of England as well as Scotland. Thus Scotland asserted not only her own right to remain a monarchy, but her determination to reimpose her native dynasty on England. The young Charles II was brought back to Scotland from exile in the Netherlands after signing the Covenants. At first he was kept virtually a prisoner, while the Kirk Party tried to mould him into a godly covenanted king. But his return to Scotland provoked English invasion, and the Kirk Party's purged, godly army was routed at the Battle of Dunbar. The regime was forced to abandon Edinburgh and retreat north of the Forth.

The great disaster at Dunbar finally destroyed the Covenanting movement as a national force and ideology. Most ministers and members of Parliament concluded that in order to defeat the English it was necessary to allow the ungodly — Engagers and royalists — to fight alongside the godly. Dunbar had discredited the Kirk Party, and many Scots were coming to see the war primarily not as a religious crusade but as a national war against the centuries-old enemy: and the traditional rallying-point for such patriotic sentiment was the crown. Royalists flocked back into the army, and then into Parliament and political office. A minority of extremists in the church refused to accept the inevitable. These, the Remonstrants or Protesters, would not submit to the decision to compromise (by abandoning purging) made by the Resolutioner majority in the church. In practice (though they would have denied it) these extremists virtually seceded and formed their own church: indeed for a few months they maintained an autonomous army, that of the Western Association, fighting the English but virtually disowning the king in doing so, in the belief that this would bring them God's favour.

By mid-1651 royalists had in effect ousted the Covenanters from power. For many, perhaps most, Scots the Covenants were discredited, having brought repeated disasters on the country. Resistance to the English was the priority as a great royalist-nationalist revival swept the country. The Engagers in 1648 had attempted a limited counter-revolution, but it was in 1651 that counter-revolution finally triumphed. Before the implications of this could be worked out, however, the regime collapsed in the face of English armies, a despairing invasion of England leading to another massive defeat at the Battle of Worcester.

Scotland was a conquered country. Her attempts to assert her identity and secure her future within Britain had seemed to the English to be repeated interference in English affairs. This had provoked English conquest and thereafter an 'incorporating' union in which the Scottish Parliament was abolished. The intoxicating concepts enshrined in the National Covenant had led to disaster and despair.

7

The Later Covenanters, 1651-90

THE KIRK PARTY, and indeed the whole Covenanting movement, had collapsed in a welter of arguments and recriminations as the English conquered the country in 1650-1. These quarrels, dividing the church into bitterly feuding factions, continued for the rest of the 1650s, the decade of English rule. For the great majority of nobles and lairds the Covenants were dead, disastrous mistakes that had led to chaos, defeat and threats to the established social hierarchy. Many in the lower levels of society probably had similar views, while others would still have maintained that the Covenants had represented a noble and worthy dream while admitting that they had failed and that in changed circumstances they were no longer relevant. But for others, including at first virtually all the ministers of the church, the Covenants represented a perpetual, unbreakable national obligation — though with the country occupied by an English army and the church divided into bitterly opposed parties arguing interminably about whose fault the collapse of the cause had been, the antics of the ministers were of little consequence.

Eventually in 1660 monarchy, and with it the Union of the Crowns, was restored through political developments in England. Some of the small minority which formed the extremist Protester faction in the church recalled that Charles II had himself signed the Covenants in 1650, and hoped that he would still feel bound by them. The great majority of ministers, however, were ready quietly to abandon them, recognising (however reluctantly) that some compromise in religion was necessary. In the general mood of fervent loyalty to the crown, the desperate hope was that after years of disaster and conquest the monarchy could revive Scotland's fortunes. The Covenants were an embarrassment, a reminder that it had been events in Scotland which had begun the process which had led to revolution in all three kingdoms. Most hoped that a modified Presbyterianism, tacitly accepting subordination to the crown, could be retained: but when the king decreed that bishops were to return, and he and Parliament outlawed the Covenants, this was accepted with sad resignation. It was no use looking to the nobility, who had taken the lead in overthrowing Episcopacy a generation before: the attack on their position by the Kirk Party had frightened them back into suspicious hostility to Presbyterianism as dangerous to social order.

For some ministers, however, acceptance of Episcopacy was impossible, though at first it looked as if this irreconcilable minority would be a small one. But Charles II's ministers blundered over the details of the church settlement. An act restoring lay patronage, the right of the crown or individual landlords in most parishes to appoint the parish ministers, contained retrospective clauses which suggested that many ministers had been irregularly appointed and thus would not become true ministers of the church until they got the restored patrons to present them to their parishes. Worse, such ministers would also have to go to bishops to ask them to regularise their positions. Thus hundreds of ministers, most of whom had reluctantly decided to accept the return of bishops, calculating that they were distant officials they could try to avoid having anything to do with, were faced with the humiliating prospect of having to admit the irregularity of their appointments to the ministry, and individually and directly accept the power of bishops over them. This was the last straw for many, and within a few years over a quarter of the ministers of the Church of Scotland were deposed from the ministry, the majority of them for refusing to accept this aspect of the Restoration church settlement.

More important than the number of ministers deposed was the fact that many of them retained the loyalty of substantial proportions of their former congregations. Under the leadership of some of the 'outed' ministers a major problem of religious dissent therefore emerged, concentrated on parts of the western and south western Lowlands, the areas that had been the heartland of the Covenanting cause ever since 1638.

The dissenters of the Restoration period are usually referred to as the later Covenanters but, especially at first, many did not openly support the Covenants. Nor at first is it entirely accurate to call the movement Presbyterian, for some would have been willing to accept moderate Episcopacy, even if with some reluctance. Thus it is perhaps best to label them conventiclers: the dissidence problem centred on the attempts of the regime to force people to attend the services of the established church, while such 'non-conformists' fought to maintain their own illegal worship, the conventicles. Yet though there was thus a wide range of standpoints among the dissidents, varying degrees of passive or active resistance supported by different individuals at different times, at the core of the movement lay devotion to Presbyterian principles and, increasingly as time passed, open support for the Covenants.

The attempts of the government to restore religious uniformity backfired disastrously. Clumsy persecution through the army was meant to prevent trouble: instead it provoked a rebellion in which several thousand westerners took part in 1666. Briefly this caused panic: was this 1637-8 all over again? But in reality the situation was very different, and the isolated rebels were easily defeated at the Battle of Rullion Green when they advanced towards Edinburgh. The landowning social élites being firmly behind the king, there was no possibility of a great national movement based on religious grievances in the 1660s. The rebels of 1666 were overwhelmingly men of humble social status, peasant farmers and the like, with the leadership and encouragement of a few former ministers and minor landlords. As in 1638 religious issues were not all that was at stake: behind the 1666 rising lay also secular grievances at high taxation, insensitive absentee government, and subordination of Scottish interests to English ones (Scotland had been dragged into a war with the Dutch which was regarded as being English in its motivation). But though Scots in general might grumble at such things they were determinedly obedient to the crown. With the terrible memories of what defiance to it had led to a generation before in their minds, rebellion was unthinkable.

The rebels of 1666 had appealed to the Covenants (and like the 1638 predecessors had insisted on their loyalty to the crown, in spite of appearances to the contrary). Though their rebellion was only a minor and pale reflection of its predecessor, it was of great interest in one respect. In 1638 the people of Scotland had followed the example of their customary leaders, the nobility and other landowners, in acting against the king. The 1666 rebels, on the other hand, had defied not just the state but their social superiors. Thus though it was small in scale, the rising has significance in that it has been hailed as the first popular rising in Scottish history (Rosalind Mitchison). In fact one predecessor can be claimed: in 1648 several thousand westerners had gathered to defy the Engagers as betrayers of the cause of the Covenants, in spite of the fact that their noble leaders failed to provide leadership, only to be dispersed at a skirmish at Mauchline Moor.

In the Reformation of 1560 the Scots who formed the forces of the Lords of the Congregation had fought over-whelmingly because their landlords told them to. In the years after 1638 most of those in the Covenanters' armies had also done their landlords' bidding, but there was genuine popular enthusiasm for the cause of true religion as well, inspired by the ministers of the church. The ministers, especially in the south-west, were coming to wield influence over the behaviour of the commons to rival that of landlords, on occasion indeed supplanting it, as when the teaching of the church inspired men to ignore or defy the wishes of royalist landlords.

Now, in 1666, a rebellion had taken place in which most of those involved put what they saw as the interests of true religion first, leaving landlords helpless. These developments might be seen as a crude index of the increasing hold of a new ideology over some sections of the common people, Protestant teaching weakening or breaking ingrained habits of social deference by urging that personal responsibility to God must over-ride obedience to one's betters. Of course it would be folly to hail this uncritically as a 'progressive' development: automatic deference to superiors was being replaced by unquestioning obedience to fanatical, narrow religious dogmas imposed from above by ministers. Modern eyes may see the two alternatives, of social deference or religious fanaticism, as equally unattractive, but what was significant was not what the alternatives were, but that there *were* alternatives. The fact that men had to choose between the dictates of landlords and of religion meant that, whatever decision they reached, they had had to debate (in their own minds or with others) the question of where ultimate authority lay.

The events of 1666 demonstrated that the Covenanting cause was no longer that of the nation as a whole, but merely that of a limited number of people mainly of humble status. This led inevitably to major changes in the Covenanting tradition. The National Covenant had first been known as the Noblemen's Covenant, and covenanting ministers had acknowledged this by styling the nobility Christ's nobility, not just the king's. Church and nobility had combined to impose godly reformation on the population as a whole. The 'desertion' of most of the nobility to join the Engagers in 1648 had shattered this dominant social conservatism within the Covenanting movement: the nobility had betrayed God, the common people were after all the true people of God. The experience of the Restoration period confirmed this change.

The rulers of society — corrupt both in their public policies and in their personal lives — had abandoned the cause of God and were trying to destroy it by tyrannical persecution of the people. Only the commons were now prepared to stand for the godly cause, and as a result they were suffering brutal oppression.

The Restoration regime has a bad reputation, and rightly so, for its attempts to enforce religious conformity. Yet it did intersperse persecution with concessions and offers of compromise which, given the circumstances, were at times quite generous and showed a degree of flexibility. The Indulgences of 1669 and 1672 tried to attract men back into the established church on easy terms, and a significant number of dissidents accepted them. But on the whole concessions were too little and too late. The experience of persecution, as so often happens, embittered many of the victims and drove them to take up harder, more extreme, positions than those they had maintained in the past. Fearing a collapse of royal authority in much of the west in particular, the government felt it necessary to intensify persecution of conventiclers. The result was another rebellion, sparked off by the assassination of the Archbishop of St Andrews (itself of course a symptom of the growing fanaticism of some of the dissidents) and victory over a detachment of troops at the Battle of Drumclog in 1679. Again rebellion was easily defeated, at the Battle of Bothwell Bridge. In the aftermath of that defeat a new Indulgence offered, with remarkable generosity, not a way of rejoining the establishment but toleration outside it for 'house conventicles' — small indoor Presbyterian services — in most of the country, provided the Privy Council was satisfied that the preachers conducting the services could be trusted not to stir up trouble.

At first it looked as if the problem of dissent might at last have been solved. The 1679 rebellion had been inspired by hopes that the moment had come when God would help his chosen people to destroy enemies. Defeat showed that this was not the case. The result was intense demoralisation among the dissidents — though most of them had taken no active part in the rising. Most seemed ready to accept limited toleration for worship outside the Church of Scotland. It meant the abandonment of great dreams of overthrowing the Episcopalian establishment, but it was better than nothing.

A few, however, would not submit. In 1666 the rebels had claimed to fight for king and Covenants, as in 1638. By 1679 some extreme dissidents who still maintained the Covenants were increasingly and openly critical of the monarchy which had caused so much suffering by persecuting those standing for the cause of God. While not attacking the institution of monarchy, they were prepared to admit they were fighting the king's own policies. To men of such views mere toleration was not enough: acceptance of it would amount to defeat. The fight must be carried on to complete victory, which would surely come in the end through divine intervention, whatever the odds in worldly terms.

The more isolated these fanatics became, as conventiclers of more moderate views submitted, the more extreme were the ideas they expressed. Ever wilder rhetoric was needed to bolster their confidence. In the so-called 'Queensferry Paper' of 1680, for example, they explained how they were bound by 'our national covenants' to overthrow the kingdom of darkness, by the Solemn League and Covenant to destroy superstition and Episcopacy. As the hands of their kings and rulers were against the throne of the Lord, the Lord had declared war on them for ever and commanded his people 'utterly to root them out'. Monarchy had declined from virtue, moderation and good government to idle and sinful magnificence, absolute and tyrannical 'to keep on a yoke of thraldom upon the subjects, and to squeeze from them their substance to uphold their lustful and pompous superfluities'. It could no longer be called a government but 'a lustful rage'. The godly were therefore freed from any obligation to the crown, and should bind themselves together to defend their 'natural, civil and divine rights and liberties'. Later the same year the preacher Richard Cameron (soon to be killed in a skirmish at Airds Moss) and his tiny band of supporters went even further in the 'Sanquhar Declaration'. Describing themselves as 'the representatives of the true Presbyterian church and covenanted nation of Scotland', they argued that Charles II should have been removed from his throne for his breaches of the Covenants and other sins, and declared war on him under 'our Lord Jesus Christ, Captain of Salvation' as a tyrant and usurper

A few reacted to persecution not with aggressive declarations but eccentric and mystical withdrawal from the mainstream conflict: John Gibb, a ship's captain, and his little band of adherents (mainly women) in 1681 gave up work to fast, pray and sing psalms. All took Biblical names (Gibb becoming King Solomon !), and the main persecution they, the 'sweet singers of Israel', suffered at first was from irate husbands trying to reclaim their wives. Eventually imprisoned, Gibb and his male followers drew up a 'covenant' rejecting most aspects of conventional religious practice, all previous covenants, King Charles and all other tyrants, the names of the months and of the days of the week, and a good deal more.

Such peculiarities posed no threat to the country's rulers, but to the Cameronians' declaration of war the government inevitably replied with war. The enemy was intended to be the tiny number of fanatics, but attempts to destroy them by military repression were clumsy and bungling. The state experienced the same problem as some modern regimes trying to deal with extremist minority guerilla movements, and in particular the difficulty of catching the real activists when they (in the south-west at least) swam in the sea of a peasantry who though outwardly submissive to the regime had some sympathy with the rebels and would not cooperate in hunting them down. The Restoration regime's forces made the same mistakes as those often seen today. Frustrated by being unable to catch their real enemies, they tried to isolate them by action against their families and against those suspected of helping rebels by giving them food or lodging. Such attempts to isolate the extremists from the rest of the population sometimes widened into attempts to terrify whole communities into refusing to help them in any way. Thus what should ideally have been a precise surgical operation against isolated and fanatical rebels grew into indiscriminate persecution in many areas, with the inevitable result of driving increasing numbers into active support for the fanatics. The 1680s became the 'Killing Times' of later Presbyterian mythology. By modern standards, perhaps, bloodshed and atrocity were very limited. But it is clear that suffering was widespread, and the summary executions without trial of men who refused to disown the most extreme beliefs of the fanatics left an indelible mark on the folk memories of the people. The 'blood sacrifice' of these martyrs was never to be forgotten.

Even many who had no sympathy with the views of the extremists were worried by the excesses committed in trying to destroy them. The failure of the Restoration regime to solve the problem of religious dissent was disillusioning to many, and brutality and illegalities on the part of the army raised worries about the nature and future policies of the regime. But much greater apprehension in the country as a whole was roused by the fact that from the 1670s it was known that King Charles' brother and heir, James, Duke of York, was a Catholic. As part of a campaign to ensure his succession to the throne in spite of his religion the Test Act Oath was introduced to be taken by office-holders in Scotland. On the one hand the oath upheld Protestantism but on the other asserted the power of the crown and its unalterable hereditary descent, and denounced the Covenants. The oath was badly worded, and many felt that it was ambiguous and inconsistent. About 80 ministers were deposed for refusing to take it. Protestants of all shades of

opinion were now worried about the future, and this
intensified when the duke came to the throne in 1685 as James
VII. His favour to Catholics and attempts to encourage
conversions to his own faith led to growing alarm.
Presbyterians had long argued that Episcopacy was inevitably
a half-way house on the road to Catholicism: events now
seemed to be proving them right. James might argue that he
only wanted toleration for his co-religionists, and that he
would tolerate moderate Protestant dissenters as well, but his
religious policies and arbitrary style of government, recalling
that of his father Charles I, made many fear that the
destruction of Protestantism was being plotted. Nothing but
such a revived Catholic threat could have made
Presbyterianism respectable again in the élites of society which
had so decisively rejected it after the failures of the early
Covenanters in the 1640s.

Nonetheless, apart from the fanatics in the west, the Scots
were not prepared to defy their king: the desperate reliance on
the monarchy as the only hope of stability, engendered by the
disasters which had followed on opposing Charles I, was still
strong. That episode had also proved that for the Scots to try
to take an initiative in British affairs was likely to lead to
disaster. Thus it was that the Revolution of 1688 which
overthrew King James, like the Restoration of monarchy in
1660, was made in England and then tamely accepted by
Scotland: it was hardly a 'Glorious Revolution' north of the
border.

The Scottish ruling élites had not made the revolution, but
they hastened to accept it once it triumphed in England, and
like the English accepted the dethroned king's daughter,
Mary, and her Dutch husband William of Orange, as their
new joint sovereigns. But what of religion? William would
have been happy to retain Episcopacy in Scotland, as was done
in England. Political circumstances made this impossible,
however. The Scots bishops and the great majority of the
Episcopalian clergy remained loyal to King James, refusing to

accept William as rightful king, whereas many of William's most fervent supporters were Presbyterians. Moreover in the west in many parishes news of the Revolution had sparked off spontaneous action, with triumphant Presbyterian mobs driving hated Episcopalian ministers out. It was quite clear that any attempt to reinstate such ministers would meet with violent opposition, and William had no wish thus to perpetuate the running sore of religious conflict in the west which had done so much to discredit the Restoration regime over three decades. Out of political expediency, therefore, Presbyterianism was restored in 1690. It was said that this was 'agreeable to the inclinations of the people' — but as they were not consulted it is impossible to know whether this was true or not.

Presbyterianism was restored: the Covenants were not. The new established church that emerged represented a compromise in which the Covenants, the old exclusive claims for Presbyterianism as the only godly form of church government, and insistence on independence from state influence, were abandoned. Theoretical claims to independence might still be asserted from time to time. Some ministers at least looked back to the great Covenants with nostalgia and pride, and those who had suffered and died in 1660-88 were hailed as martyrs whose cause had now at last triumphed. But these were merely sentimental dreams of past glory, and it was generally accepted that in practice the National Covenant and Solemn League and Covenant had no direct application to circumstances several generations later. Yet the story of Scotland's Covenants was far from ended.

8

The Legacy of the Covenants

TO THE GREAT majority of Scottish Presbyterians the post-1690 compromise in the established church was acceptable. To a small minority it was not. To abandon the full claims of Presbyterianism and the Covenants was an ungodly betrayal. These folk were the surviving extremists of the Killing Times of the 1680s and their heirs. Yet they too accepted compromise in some respects. Though they denounced the Presbyterian establishment for its defections they accepted tacit toleration outside it. They maintained that they were the only true church of God in the country, and might have distant dreams of ultimately triumphing nationally. But in practice they settled down as small, isolated sects, instead of maintaining the war on their enemies. The regimes of King William and his successors and the form of the established church might be unsatisfactory. They were, however, a lot better than a Catholic king and an Episcopalian church, and a destructive war among Presbyterians might weaken the government and lead to the return of the Catholic James VII.

This minority had already formed itself into little prayer societies in the years before the 1688 revolution, and from these organisations members became known as the Society People. An alternative name was Cameronians, in recognition of Richard Cameron's contribution to their outlook. With their narrow, exclusive views the Cameronians proved remarkably prone to schism, as tiny groups of men and women broke away under their own leaders, but the mainstream survived to constitute itself the Reformed Presbyterian Church in the mid eighteenth century, still steadfast in its adherence to the Covenants. So too were the splinter groups, though many were short-lived, like the 'Howdenites'. These followers of one John Howden declared war on 'the Turk, the Pope and the Prelates' in 1739, 'the first year of our Covenanted States'. Ten years later they were describing themselves as 'the most Serene and most Potent in the Lord, the Covenanted States of the Commonwealth of Scotland', with Christ as their only king and head of state.

This sort of bombast invites ridicule. Yet even the most absurd of such groups illustrate an important point. In the seventeenth century the preaching of Presbyterian ministers had on occasion persuaded men to ignore their duties to their social superiors, and instead to give first priority to their obligations to God under the Covenants, but when this happened the unquestioned authority of the minister had been substituted for that of the landlord. By this time, however, under the influence of aspects of Protestant teaching that stressed that it was essential for all to seek to read and understand the Bible for themselves, to take responsibility for their own consciences, their own personal relationship with God, ordinary Scots men and women were increasingly willing to go further and to defy simultaneously both landlords and ministers they disagreed with. The point was, indeed, illustrated by events in 1690. The three ministers who had been leading the Cameronians up to this time all agreed to serve the established church now that Presbyterianism had been restored: but few members of their congregations followed their lead. As the history of the Cameronians and later secessions from the establishment demonstrated, a new self-reliance and confidence was emerging among common folk, especially in the west, displayed in a willingness and ability to think for themselves and express their opinions. Visitors were by the later eighteenth century remarking on a peasantry fascinated by theological debate and enjoying involvement in argument on controversial points, with a rich store of biblical knowledge to draw on. It is true that much of such debate was bigoted and narrow, but the power to reason, the confidence to debate and uphold opinions, spread skills which could also be applied to other aspects of life than religion, and these skills were to be an important legacy for the future, when social and economic change led to the slow development of working class organisation.

Like virtually all the minority groups which have since taken strength from the Covenanters of the seventeenth century, the Cameronians and their offshoots identified with the later rather than the early Covenanters, with the Covenanters as the poor, suffering, despised remnant of the true church rather than the Covenanters led by the nobility in the arrogance of their days in power in the 1640s, zealously persecuting others. To the Reformed Presbyterians their isolation made their continued testimony to the Covenants all the more important. On occasions of what they perceived as crisis they would gather to renew the Covenants. Thus in 1712 after an act granting limited toleration to some Episcopalians had been passed by Parliament they assembled at Auchensauch (near Douglas in Lanarkshire) to reaffirm their obligations, and at Crawfordjohn (Lanarkshire) in 1745 they again publicly renewed the Covenants. This was the last formal renewal, but their adherence to the Covenants was repeatedly asserted in the generations that followed — as in their 1761 'Act, Declaration, and Testimony for the whole of the Covenanted Reformation'.

The Cameronians had another institutional legacy apart from the Reformed Presbyterian Church. Those who had risen in arms to support the Revolution of 1688 formed what became known as the Cameronian Regiment. This received its baptism of fire in the fighting in Dunkeld which halted the advance south of the forces of the dethroned James VII. The regiment became part of the British Army, and right up until its disbandment in 1968 it retained customs commemorating its origins in the armed conventicles of the Restoration period: during church services members of the regiment carried arms, and guards were posted, as though the forces of an ungodly government were still scouring the hills in pursuit of the Covenanters.

In time other Presbyterian groups joined the Cameronians in making the Covenants symbols of hope and righteousness in times of suffering (even if the suffering only consisted of inability to accept the established church). Ministers who withdrew from the established Church of Scotland in 1733 claimed to stand for 'the true Presbyterian Covenanted Church of Scotland'. In 1737 their new Secession Church asserted the perpetual obligations on Scotland of the National Covenant and the Solemn League and Covenant, and acceptance of the Covenants became a condition for admission to communion. In 1743 (the centenary of the Solemn League and Covenant) after a sermon on 'Covenanted Grace for Covenanting Work' a new band was sworn upholding the Covenants — though this band later (1777) brought denunciations from the Cameronians as it implied that the Covenants needed interpreting to apply them to the circumstances of the age.

The Cameronians provided a church for a small number of extremists: the new Secession Church by contrast grew by the end of the eighteenth century to a strength of perhaps 150,000. Its many congregations offered Presbyterians a mainline alternative to the establishment, thus further encouraging popular intellectual debate, the exercise of the duty to study the Scriptures and decide for oneself which of the brands of Presbyterianism on offer was the more godly.

Through the self-pitying identification of Presbyterian groups outside the establishment with the sufferings of the later Covenanters, the memory of the latter remained strong. In the eighteenth and early nineteenth centuries an extensive popular literature evolved, surrounding the martyrs with a severe romantic glamour. Much of this hagiographical literature was uncritical, but it was largely derived from

Robert Wodrow's *The History of the Sufferings of the Church of Scotland from the Restoration to the Revolution*, first published in 1722. Scholarly to the extent that it was based on documentary sources, but one-sided in its interpretations, this work sought to denounce the persecutions of Presbyterians on the one hand, while on the other rejecting the excesses of fanatics like the Cameronians: Wodrow 'regretted the manifold temptations poor ignorant people had at this time, to run to enthusiasm and ravery upon the one hand, and atheism and irreligion upon the other'. Thus the Church of Scotland (in which Wodrow was a minister) could claim to have arisen from the sufferings of the 1660-88 period, drawing strength and legitimacy from this, while at the same time deprecating 'enthusiasm' as something understandable as a reaction to persecution yet unjustified. In this way the established church as much as the various secession groups claimed descent from those who had suffered in the decades before 1688. Wodrow's pious volumes became the standard account of the Covenanting movement for Presbyterians of all social ranks for generations — and contributed much to the tendency to concentrate on the later Covenanters and largely ignore the early Covenanters who had actually ruled Scotland after 1638.

In spite of Wodrow's efforts, however, sympathy for the Covenanters above the popular level in society was limited. Attitudes within the establishment were ambiguous, hailing the Covenants and those who had suffered for them in their seventeenth-century context but denying their relevance in the eighteenth. The eighteenth-century social élites were increasingly proud of their rationality, their enlightenment, their escape from a discredited past into an age of improvement and progress. Rejoicing in their deliverance from persecution and bigotry, from fanaticism and its consequences, they found the martyrs of the late Covenanting period profoundly unattractive in many respects — men of extreme, narrow views, and usually of low birth and little education. They might be accepted as martyrs, but nonetheless they were regarded as having been often mistaken in their views and actions. Certainly they were not heroes to be emulated. Wodrow would have agreed, but urged the distinction between such fanatics and the mainstream Presbyterians who were being persecuted in the same period. For many in the eighteenth and early nineteenth centuries, however, the distinction was too subtle: the noisy fanatics were seen as typical of a whole discredited age.

Moreover the actions of those in the eighteenth century who identified fully with the Covenanters indicated that Covenanting ideology was still potentially dangerous. The wilder statements of the continuing Cameronian congregations branded them as unrepentant leftovers from past conflicts best forgotten. When in the 1720s many tenant farmers in Galloway were evicted, as landlords switched from emphasis on arable to pastoral farming, a sort of popular rising took place to smash down the dykes dividing up the new enclosed fields for cattle. The 'Levellers of Galloway' (so called as they 'levelled' the dykes which symbolised their grievances) as part of their protest renewed the Solemn League and Covenant. The gesture was totally irrelevant to their economic grievances, but it was a sign of how deeply the Covenanting mythology was now embedded in popular culture in the west. Clearly for these men the Covenants meant the people's cause, as opposed to that of the corrupt and oppressive upper classes.

The Covenants had spoken, though in general terms, of civil as well as religous liberties and rights, and this meant that the heritage of Covenanting history and mythology could be exploited in pursuit of causes which were not religious, by men who were not necessarily inspired by religion. The Galloway Levellers were doubtless sincere in seeing their grievances in a religious context, but in time others recognised the value of the Covenanting legacy though they rejected its bigotry. Robert Burns might spurn

Presbyterian orthodoxy on occasion, but he could nonetheless write

> *The Solemn League and Covenant*
> *Now brings a smile, now brings a tear.*
> *But sacred Freedom, too, was theirs:*
> *If thou'rt a slave, indulge thy sneer.*

Thus he could recognise the folly, and be aware that the Covenanters fought for 'liberty' to impose their own narrow religion on others. Yet still they were in some sense a part of the struggle for freedom in a wider sense, and thus demanded respect. How to interpret the fact that Burns named his favourite mare 'Jenny Geddes' after the supposed initiator of the 1637 riot in St Giles is rather more difficult, but this too may perhaps be seen as a gesture of respect!

Thus it was natural that the Covenanting tradition, so deeply rooted in many parts of the country, had a part to play in the development of working-class organisation and agitation for democratic political reform from the late eighteenth century, though this is a matter that has been little investigated. The Friends of the People in the 1790s, inspired by the French Revolution, had a number of committed Covenanters, in the form of Secession ministers, among their leading members. The government of the day tended to assume that all Seceders were potentially seditious — though in fact the Secession churches as such did not support democratic demands.

Involvement of some Seceders with popular political agitation in the 1790s revealed one major limitation in exploiting the Covenanting tradition in such a context: as it was an exclusively Presbyterian tradition placing too much stress on it was likely to be divisive, and there was therefore a tendency to relegate it to the background. Nonetheless, the Covenanting past could on occasion be exploited directly. In 1815 thousands of 'democrats', mainly textile workers engaged in industrial agitation, marched to the battlefield of Drumclog to commemorate the victory obtained by their ancestors over the government and their social superiors — and to celebrate the news of Napoleon's escape from Elba! Later, in the 1830s and 1840s, some of those involved in the Chartist movement drew inspiration from the Covenanters. Historians have commented on the fact that whereas English radicals of the period concentrated their attack on the commercial and industrial middle classes, Scottish radical agitation aimed most of its invective at the landed classes. It seems likely that this was an echo of the Covenanting past: it had provided the Scots with a strong tradition of denouncing corrupt and oppressive landlords, blaming them for the evils of society, which could be adapted and applied to a new industrial age.

By the early nineteenth century perceptions of the Covenanting legacy were altering in an age of growing popular agitation. They were altering in other ways as well. Perhaps because the Covenanting movement was now safely in the distant past, men of status and education now seemed ready to take an increasing interest in it, seeing it as a fascinating episode in the country's past, rather than dismissing it as simply an unedifying display of deplorable (though perhaps well-intentioned) fanaticism. Further, the continuing popular dedication to the memory of the Covenanting martyrs made investigating them of more than merely antiquarian interest.

The link between the popular culture concerning the Covenanters on the one hand and intellectual circles on the other is epitomised by Robert Paterson, who died in 1801. His practical contribution to keeping the memory of past suffering and sacrifice alive was to travel round the country for over forty years repairing the monuments set up to commemorate the Covenanting martyrs. This eccentric figure's devout obsession with the dead earned him the nickname of 'Old Mortality'. Walter Scott had met this old

Cameronian, and his story provided Scott with a theme and title for his novel *Old Mortality* (1816). Set mainly in the later Covenanting period, it displayed on the one hand Scott's disdain for the Covenanters (in a letter he referred to 'the beastly covenanters' who 'hardly had any claim to be called men'), but on the other it showed a recognition of their sufferings and their sincerity, made a real attempt to understand their psychology and motivation, and acknowledged their struggle as contributing to the coming of the 'Glorious' Revolution of 1688-9. Thus, like Burns, Scott disapproved of much about the Covenanters, but nonetheless he accepted that there were elements of value and interest in their legacy. Thomas Carlyle, brought up on popular Covenanting tales, displayed a similar ambiguity in his attitude to the movement (in his *On Heroes and Hero Worship*). Intolerant popular fanaticism had contributed to the achievement of 'liberty':

> A tumult in the High Church of Edinburgh spread into a universal battle and struggle in all these realms; there came out, after fifty years' struggling, what we call the *Glorious* Revolution, a *Habeas-Corpus* Act, Free Parliaments, and much else. . . .

Brilliantly characterising the people's contribution to a revolution which in the event benefited mainly their genteel social betters, Carlyle asked how many

> Earnest rugged Cromwells, Knoxes, poor Peasant Covenants, wrestling, battling for very life, in rough mirey places, have to struggle, and suffer, and fall, greatly censured, *bemired*, — before a beautiful Revolution of Eighty-eight can step-over them in official pumps and silk-stockings?

Despite its insights, Scott's *Old Mortality* became a centre of controversy immediately on publication, as those steeped in Covenanting mythology denounced the author for not being one hundred per cent on their side. Much more acceptable in their eyes was James Hogg's *The Brownie of Bodsbeck* —

published in 1818 though it may have been written before Scott's work. Hogg was fully committed to the Covenanting side, though recognising the fanaticism involved. Scott chided Hogg for his unfair, one-sided interpretation of the past: Hogg replied indignantly 'It is the picture I hae been bred up in the belief o' sin' ever I was born'. Scott had tried to be fair according to his lights; Hogg was proud of his one-sided approach arising from the popular Covenanting tradition. Moreover, claimed Hogg, all his incidents were based on fact 'And that's a great deal mair than you can say for your tale o' Auld Mortality'!

John Galt, Scotland's third notable novelist of the age, also entered the fray provoked by Scott's supposedly irreverent treatment of the Covenanters. His *Ringan Gilhaize, or, the Covenanters* (1823) traces the struggles of the Gilhaize family from before the Reformation of 1560 to after the 1688 Revolution. The central themes are the struggle for religious and other liberties, and the corrupt abuse of power by church, state, and social élites. In this epic contest between good and evil the struggle becomes increasingly bitter and socially divisive as the great men who originally led the godly cause desert it, leaving the people to fight on alone. Generations of the family's sufferings are at last given meaning and purpose when in 1689 Ringan Gilhaize is the man who shoots John Graham of Claverhouse, Lord Dundee, on the battlefield of Killiecrankie, thus thwarting his attempt to restore the Catholic tyrant James VII to the throne. God's providential purpose in preserving the Gilhaizes through their struggles is thus revealed. 'The fortunes of the papistical Stuarts are foundered for ever. Never again in this land shall any king, of his own caprice and prerogative, dare to violate the conscience of the people'.

Victory in this little literary contest over the Covenanters lay with Scott: the work of Hogg and Galt attracted comparatively little attention — perhaps because they basically accepted the prevailing orthodoxy in interpreting the movement while Scott had challenged it. In the same period as the Covenanters earned the respectability of being regarded as suitable subjects for literary treatment, they were gaining in respectability in other ways as well. Increasingly many within the Church of Scotland were coming to the conclusion that the church had betrayed its Presbyterian principles by accepting subordination to the state, especially over the patronage system whereby most parish ministers were appointed by landlords, the opinions of congregations being largely ignored. Unease and indignation swelled into a massive dispute over whether the church's freedom of action could be curtailed by decisions of Parliament and the law courts. The 'Ten Years' Conflict' which followed culminated in the Disruption of 1843.

For generations the Church of Scotland as a whole had tended to treat the Covenants as things which might have had some validity in a past age but which were no longer relevant. In the General Assembly in 1723 when a speaker had mentioned them, the moderator had intervened to state specifically that the church was no longer on 'the footing of the Covenants', and to the 'Moderate' faction, which had dominated the church in the second half of the eighteenth century, the battle for the Covenants typified a ferocious and barbarous past age. To their Evangelical opponents, humiliated by the church's subservience to the state's laws, the Covenants had more appeal, and the demands for true Presbyterianism free from state control which were made during the Ten Years' Conflict inevitably led to the revival of memories of the Covenants as being concerned with such issues. Thus when at the Disruption over a third of the establishment's ministers seceded to form the Free Church of Scotland it was hardly surprising to find the new church declaring its adherence to the 'National Covenant' of 1581 (in reality, of course, the Negative Confession), as renewed in 1638, and the Solemn League and Covenant. That the Disruption occurred in the year of the two hundreth anniversary of the Solemn League and Covenant doubtless intensified this identification of the Free Church with the Covenanters' struggles.

The identification was, however, more symbolic than real: the details of the Covenants of 1638 and 1643 had little to offer the Free Church and received little attention. But the concept of these documents as perpetually binding on the people of God helped give the new Free Church historical legitimacy by placing it in the context of the country's past. The intense controversy surrounding the Disruption led to a remarkable growth in popular works on the Covenants: of more permanent value, however, the revived interest in them also encouraged serious historical scholarship and the publication of many sources relating to the period.

To this day some of Scotland's smaller Presbyterian churches maintain their allegiance to the Covenants, and even those which do not are still influenced in their outlooks by the Covenanting legacy. Eighteenth- and nineteenth-century works which celebrate the heroes of the Covenants in the most indiscriminate and uncritical ways are still occasionally reprinted.

If support for the religious aspects of the Covenanting movement's message survived through the nineteenth century and into the twentieth, so too did other interpretations seeing the struggle as one for liberty, as a popular struggle against oppression, and as a national struggle. James Keir Hardie, founder of the Scottish Labour Party in 1888 and four years later Britain's first Labour MP, was deeply conscious of the Covenanting heritage of his Lanarkshire ancestors. After his death Ramsay MacDonald wrote

> If Hardie had ever written a historical introduction to a history of the Labour Movement, he would not have begun with the Reform Bill or any such insignificant superficiality, but with Airds Moss, the Declaration of Sanquhar, and that time and such happenings.

And it has been suggested that Keir Hardie's intolerance and unbending character owed something to his Covenanting heroes!

The ghosts of the Covenanting martyrs can also be detected in the ancestry of the 'Red Clydeside' of the 1910s and 1920s. Among the 'red' politicians of the day, and in the literature they produced, identification of the working class struggle with that of the oppressed later Covenanters was commonplace. In 1920 the Scottish Labour Housing Association organised resistance to rent increases, enshrining its standpoint in a 'Solemn League and Covenant': here the identification of the oppressors of the people as landlords in the Covenanting tradition could be usefully employed, a little ingenuity diverting the bitterness originally directed at rural landowners to the owners of urban working-class housing. At the extraordinary demonstration in Glasgow on the occasion of the departure of the victorious Clydesider MPs for Parliament (after they had signed a declaration 'breathing the noble spirit of the Covenant') the 124th psalm, 'Scotland's psalm of deliverance' was sung in the version used by the Covenanters in the seventeenth century. But those involved represented the 'last generation of working-class Scots for whom nineteenth-century Presbyterian theological controversy still lived' (Iain McLean), and as increasingly the substantial Catholic minority in the Scottish working classes became active in radical politics appeals to Covenants originally aimed at the extermination of Catholicism became less acceptable. Further, most of these Catholics were of Irish descent. To them the word 'covenant' might well evoke the Ulster Covenant of 1912 whereby the Protestant unionists of the north of Ireland had bound themselves to resist Home Rule for Ireland. As this had led to the partition of Ireland any Labour politician trying to whip up support by recalling the Covenanting past would be likely to alienate the Irish vote in Scotland. Yet the Covenanting-socialist tradition was to linger on for decades. An outstanding example of the

combination of Christian, socialist and nationalist values was
James Barr. A United Free Presbyterian minister, he was
elected as Independent Labout Party MP for Motherwell in
1924, fought for Home Rule for Scotland, and at the end of
his political career published *The Scottish Covenanters* (1946),
his interpretation of the Covenanters' struggle as a fight by
the people against both civil and religious oppression by their
superiors.

It was the later Covenanters of the Restoration period who
provided the inspiration for working class movements, but it
was the years of Covenanting rule after 1638 and the attempts
then made to protect Scotland's identity within Britain
through a new federal union that had most to offer patriotic
movements: the Covenants not as symbols of class conflict
within Scotland but on the contrary as standing for the
unifying of men of all ranks in patriotic struggle. In 1930 the
National Party of Scotland launched 'The Covenant', in
which signatories pledged themselves to do all in their power
to restore Scotland's independence, and in 1949 the group
calling itself the Scottish Convention produced another
covenant. This document (also calling itself an Engagement,
an unfortunate term considering the effects of the 1647
Engagement in splitting the original Covenanting movement)
demanded constitutional reform to create a Scottish
parliament. Circulating for some years, it eventually collected
over two million signatures — far more than the original
National Covenant could claim! — before disappearing into
obscurity.

In Scotland since the sixteenth century two great popular
historical mythologies have emerged, often rivals but
sometimes intertwined. One has concentrated on her royal
dynasty and its sufferings, forming itself round the
dethronement and ultimate execution of Mary Queen of
Scots, the martyrdom of Charles I and his Scottish

representative the Marquis of Montrose, the unjust expulsion of James VII and the death at Killiecrankie of Graham of Claverhouse as a sacrificial offering, the Jacobite risings and Bonnie Prince Charlie, loyal Highlanders and tartan trappings, romanticism and nostalgia. The other is the Presbyterian/Covenanting tradition of struggle for religious and other freedoms, of the rights of the people and the individual conscience, of the fight against the oppressive and corrupt rulers of the land (typified by the Stuart dynasty), of poor folk hunted across the moors by brutal troopers. The original 'Noblemen's Covenant' had thus evolved into the people's Covenants, creating a tradition that has fed into working class and democratic movements.

Clearly in many respects these two traditions clash head on, but they have some common ground, sharing elements of patriotic appeal and complaint at Scotland's plight within Britain (as early as the opening years of the eighteenth century some Cameronians, extreme Presbyterians, were ready to conspire with predominantly Episcopalian and Catholic Jacobites against the government of the day). Each tradition tends to distort the past to suit its purposes, presenting images of Scotland's history which are often unreal and oversimplified. From a nationalist viewpoint their rivalry may be regretted as likely to divide and thus weaken any national movement. But on the other hand the tensions and interactions between the two traditions contribute to the complexity and fascination of Scotland's identity: both are essential to it. Whether one prefers the flashy superficiality of the royalist-Jacobite tradition or the dour and at times narrow Covenanting one which nonetheless had popular appeal and a part to play in emancipating the common people from unquestioning obedience to those set over them, is a matter of taste.

This is not the place to attempt to survey either the vast literature relating specifically to the Covenanting movement since the seventeenth century, or the many histories of Scotland (and more specifically church histories) which give a prominent place to the movement. Instead this brief bibliography will concentrate on modern studies of the movement. But for a taste of traditional Presbyterian literature on the subject the many extracts gathered in *Treasury of the Scottish Covenant*, edited by John C. Johnston (Edinburgh, 1887) is a good starting point, and an excellent survey, clear and concise, of the intricacies of Scottish church history is to be found in Gordon Donaldson, *Scotland, Church and Nation through Sixteen Centuries* (Edinburgh, 1960, 1972).

David Stevenson has attempted to provide a narrative and analysis of the Covenanting revolution in *The Scottish Revolution, The Triumph of the Covenanters, 1637-44* (Newton Abbot, 1973) and *Revolution and Counter-Revolution in Scotland, 1644-51* (London, 1977). Ian B. Cowan, *The Scottish Covenanters, 1660-88* (London, 1976) surveys the later stages of the movement. Brief but stimulating accounts of the movement can be found in Hugh Watt, *Recalling the Scottish Covenants* (London and Edinburgh, 1946) and two essays by G. D. Henderson, 'The idea of the Covenant in Scotland', in *The Burning Bush, Studies in Scottish Church History* (Edinburgh, 1957) and G. D. Henderson, 'The Covenanters', in *Religious Life in Seventeenth Century Scotland* (Cambridge, 1937). Ian B. Cowan, 'The Covenanters: A Revision Article', *Scottish Historical Review*, xlvii (1968) contains a very useful discussion of the historical literature relating to the Covenanters.

The origins of the covenant concept are examined in two papers by S. A. Burrell, 'The Covenant Idea as a Revolutionary Symbol in Scotland, 1596-1637', *Church History*, xxvii (1958) and 'The Apocalyptic Vision of the Early Covenanters', *Scottish Historical Review*, xliii (1964), J. Wormald, *Lords and Men in Scotland: Bonds of Manrent,*

1442-1603 (Edinburgh, 1985) studies the Scottish tradition of bonding to which the National Covenant owes so much, while T. M. Lindsay, 'The Covenant Theology', *British and Foreign Evangelical Review*, xxviii (1879) offers a useful introduction to federal theology. A modern theologian, J. B. Torrance, examines the same subject in 'Covenant or Contract? A Study of the Theological Background of Worship in Seventeenth-Century Scotland', *Scottish Journal of Theology*, xxiii (1970) and 'The Covenant Concept in Scottish Theology and Politics and its Legacy', *Scottish Journal of Theology*, xxxiv (1981). There is also some interesting discussion of covenant theology and its implications in Gordon Marshall, *Presbyteries and Profits, Calvinism and the Development of Capitalism in Scotland, 1560-1707* (Oxford, 1980).

D. Stevenson, 'The National Covenant: a list of known copies' will be published in *Records of the Scottish Church History Society* in 1989.

Little has been written about the legacy of the Covenanters except in purely religious terms, but a series of seminars organised by the Centre for Scottish Studies, University of Aberdeen, in 1987-8 provided stimulating papers and discussions while I was writing this pamphlet: the papers are being published: W. T. C. Brotherstone (ed.), *Traditions of Protest and Dissent in Modern Scotland from the Covenanters to Red Clydeside* (Aberdeen, 1989). One aspect of the 'legacy' is analysed in John Brims, 'The Covenanting Tradition and Scottish Radicalism in the 1790s', in *Dissent, Protest and Rebellion in Pre-Industrial Scotland* (Symposium of the Association of Scottish Historical Studies, St Andrews, 3 October 1987).